Life in a Sex-mad Society

Life in
a Sex-mad
Society

Joyce Huggett

f r a m e w o r k s

Frameworks
38 De Montfort Street,
Leicester LE1 7GP,
England

Unless otherwise stated, quotations from the Bible are from
the Holy Bible, New International Version, copyright © 1973,
1978, 1984 by the International Bible Society, New York, and
published in Great Britain by Hodder and Stoughton Ltd.

Distributed in Australia by
ANZEA Publishers.
Australian ISBN 0-85892-398-X

British Library Cataloguing in Publication Data

Hugget, Joyce *1937-*
Life in a sex-mad society.
1. Interpersonal relationships — Christian viewpoints
I. Title
248.4

ISBN 0-85110-795-8

Set in Baskerville
Typeset in Great Britain by Compuset, Belfast
Design and illustration by Spring Graphics,
Saintfield, N. Ireland
Printed in Great Britain by Collins, Glasgow.

Frameworks is an imprint of Inter-Varsity Press, the book
publishing division of the Universities and Colleges
Christian Fellowship.

Contents

Life's feast is available only to those who are willing and able to engage life on a deeply personal level, giving all, holding back nothing.

Preface

'We're very much in love. We're sorely tempted to go too far too soon physically. And we really want Jesus to be pleased with every part of our relationship. Can you help us?'

That's a question a delightful couple-in-love asked me on one occasion. And that's the question I've tried to answer throughout this book because I know that many other committed Christians are asking it too.

Space has not allowed me to do what my husband and I normally do when we speak on the subject of boy-girl relationships at conferences and in seminars: to place this question against its natural backcloth — the vocation of singleness. Instead, I have placed the spotlight on various aspects of this one question. I make no apology for doing so in this instance. In the sex-mad society in which we live, it's hard for Christians to swim against today's cultural tide and to live differently from their elders and peers. Because it's so hard, two things are vital. One is that Christian people understand what the Bible teaches about sex and relationships. The second is that they receive from God the grace and strength to live biblically. By narrowing the subject right down, I have tried to give a few key questions the time and space they deserve. It is my prayer that this treatment of the subject will result in Christians determining that, at every stage of their life, Jesus will be Lord of their relationships.

Joyce Huggett

chapter one

Should Christians pair off?

PROBLEM

'If it doesn't affect our studies, church activities and family activities very much, is it all right to go steady?'

'I've been taught that intimate boy-girl relationships are not advisable, and when I meet someone I like and would like to get to know better I feel so guilty. Should I be feeling this way?'

'Surely going out with someone is doing what comes naturally?'

'When you are a single person, what can you do about your desire for intimacy, embracing and feeling someone's skin? Is it possible to work this out in deep, platonic relationships, or isn't this a good enough reason for going out?'

These are questions young Christians often ask me. Such people seem trapped between the world's view on the one hand and the church's confused teaching on the other.

The world's view

The world bombards us with its own viewpoint on the pairing-off issue. Sometimes its message is subtle, sometimes overt, always insistent and persistent. The media — newspapers, books, advertisements, television and radio — persuade us that we should always be engaged in close relationships with the opposite sex.

The media mould

By the time they are twenty, most people today will have suffered at least half a lifetime of media

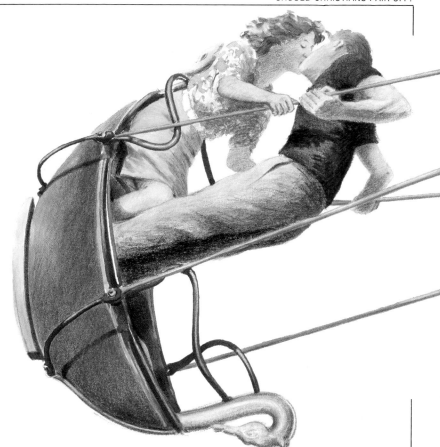

communication, urging them to indulge in intimate relationships. Almost as soon as they enter their teens, young people are put under this pressure. A mother of teenage daughters discovered this when she analysed a pile of teenage magazines one month. The nine she read had a total weekly circulation of around two million. Most of the stories focused on boy-girl relationships — falling in and out of love, jealous scheming against friends, eyeing the boy next door. They seemed to imply that all girls were interested in was boys, that sexual intercourse was all right as long as you are happy, you are not hurting another person, and a baby is not conceived by mistake.

Such a magazine produced a protest from Mrs

The message in the media is insistent and persistent . . . that we should always be engaged in close relationships with the opposite sex.

PROBLEM

Gillian Hayward in *Family* magazine, October 1985.

Jill Knight MP. When the BBC television programme *Brass Tacks* investigated the rise in schoolgirl pregnancies, she made this observation: 'Look at some of the teenage magazines read by 11- to 13-year-olds. The whole impetus and pressure in them is to suggest that really the only fun thing to do is to have sex . . . they seem to promote sex like a bar of soap . . .'

> **Safe sex can be awfully drab . . . too cosily suburban . . .**

The same message comes across strongly in magazines like the *National Student* that assume youth promiscuity. As film producer Derek Jarman said in an interview for the November 1987 issue: 'The sex scene — I don't think of it as a love scene — has a drunken impotence about it which I like; safe sex can be awfully drab . . . deep down it all seems too cosily suburban and fits too nicely — that's the right word — into the chintzy Englishness of it all. The sex in my life has been hamstrung.'

But television makes even more impact than the printed word. While the 'copycat effect' of prolonged viewing is still questioned by a minority, in a survey prepared for the Christian *Family* magazine in the spring of 1987, parents expressed the opinion that 'TV is the most significant "negative secular influence" in Great Britain today'.

Soap operas, for example, perpetuate the same myths as the teenage magazines. In an average week in Britain it is possible to spend at least ten hours watching such programmes. It is estimated that 95% of the British population have tuned into one of the series at one stage or another.

Everyone's at it!
Peer pressure is a very real problem for some young people, as Graham Turner highlighted in an article in the *Sunday Telegraph* one winter. When he talked to four girls in the top stream of a large comprehensive school, he discovered that the pressure was not simply to pair off but to do so

for one chief reason — to have sex.

'Most of the friends she went around with had already had sex, said Charlotte, aged 14. Most girls lost their virginity at 13 or 14, agreed Emma. You just had to be careful you didn't have a child and wreck your career. A lot of girls, said Helen, aged 15, felt forced into it because all their friends did it. If you were still a virgin at 13, there was something wrong with you.'

When he talked to students and student nurses, he discovered the pressure to pair off and to indulge in recreational sex was equally strong. 'Only one out of nine students I spoke to at Reading (University) disapproved of sex before marriage, two out of nine student nurses. If it was just sex you wanted, said one of the other seven, you might easily sleep with a man the first night. So long as you both knew it was a one-night stand — "and played the game," added one of her friends — there's no harm in it.'

'It was almost impossible, reported Andrew, a student in Manchester, to find a virgin these days. When he did, he added without irony and with a genuine sense of trying to be charitable, he always tried to reassure the girl that it was nothing to be ashamed of.'

> ## So long as you both knew it was a one-night stand and played the game

Graham Turner,
Sunday Telegraph,
24 February 1985

Parental pressure

Some young people even face pressure from their parents to pair off and to be promiscuous.

'I am seventeen years old and my boyfriend is eighteen. I have only been going out with him for four months and recently he has kept asking me to make love with him. I am not sure because I am still a virgin. But I have run out of excuses. I don't want to pack him up, but I am gradually going off him and I'm beginning to dread every night we go out. I spoke to my parents about it, but they said I would get asked this lots of times by boys. I told my boyfriend to look for someone else but he said he didn't want anyone but me. Every time I refuse, he sulks. My parents like him more and more. If I tell him I don't want to go out one night, my parents say I'm being nasty. I

Nottingham Trader, 23 July 1986

have tried telling them I want a break now and then, and they tell me I'm stupid.'

'Pairing off to have sex, it seems, is the norm. Indeed, it has been estimated that only 8% of brides and 7% of bridegrooms in Britain will be virgins on their wedding nights. Most claim to have had previous lovers — the national average is four but one person claimed to have had forty.'

Christians, of course, are not immune from this sexual exploitation. We are a part of the sexually supercharged climate in which we live. Conscious that Christ challenges us to be 'in the world but not of it', Christian young people look to the church and to Christian teachers for guidelines which will help them to make responsible decisions about their behaviour with friends of both sexes.

Extreme Christian reactions

'Prohibit'
So the world's message is crystal clear and powerfully insistent: 'Pair off and have sex. The

two naturally go together. What's the point of pairing off if you don't go all the way?'

But many Christians believe that sex outside marriage is wrong. We shall examine that question in chapter two. They still want to know, however — should Christians pair off? Is it right to have one steady boy/girlfriend even if we do keep out of bed?

The Christian church rightly recoils from this sex-mad society, but sometimes to extremes. The message received by young people appears to be *Don't*. This prohibition appears to apply not simply to having sex before marriage but to 'pairing off' as a principle. The implication is that boy-girl relationships which will not result in marriage are wrong.

The reasons given for this total embargo are varied:

1. They can be time-wasting, energy-sapping and heart-breaking.

2. A Christian should give his or her best years to the Lord and then start looking for a partner.

3. Touch is dangerous. Petting is like a slippery slide. Step on it and your pace accelerates faster than you imagined it would. It's better to be cautious: 'Don't squeeze me till I'm yours.'

4. If a person is at college or university, or training for a particular profession, this training must be recognized as God's revealed will for the time being. Students should concentrate on their studies wholeheartedly and wait until their course

We are part of the sexually supercharged climate in which we live.

13

PROBLEM

Idea, Autumn 1987; the quarterly bulletin of the Evangelical Alliance

is completed before they begin to look for a marriage partner.

5. The first person you go out with is the person you should marry; to have more than one partner is to dishonour God.

'Faithfulness within marriage and chastity outside continue to lose favour in Britain. Statistics show that the cost to society is high. For example, in England and Wales:

- Illegitimate births have risen 26% in 14 years.
- Four out of five conceptions to women under 20 are outside of marriage.
- More than 4,500 girls aged 15 and under become pregnant each year.'

Good relationships are essential to our sense of well-being. One reason is that men and women were made in the image of God. Among other things this means that we came into the world capable of giving and receiving love. Yet the task of making good relationships poses huge problems for many people. And when it comes to relating across the sex barrier — boy-girl relationships — the complexity of the problem increases.

'Permit'

Even more sadly, the young Christian seeking for biblical answers to the pairing-off problem will find other Christian teachers who have reacted against the prohibitionist teaching outlined above. 'What nonsense!' they say, 'Of course Christians must pair off. It's natural. It's normal. What right has anyone to spoil another person's fun?' I was once on a panel on local radio where a university chaplain expounded this philosophy most persuasively.

These teachers claim that:

1. Taboos are a thing of the past.

2. Touch in relationships is good and necessary. As long as both partners love one another, they are free to express that love in whatever way they choose so long as they don't actually indulge in the act of intercourse. Some, the more liberal, would not even draw the line at intercourse.

There is plenty of literature to support these views. Indeed, some adults give positive encouragement to young Christians to experiment sexually.

I feel uneasy about both of these extreme Christian viewpoints. The first, the prohibitionist, disturbs me because I believe that boy-girl relationships, conducted sensibly, have a value all their own. Moreover, while such relationships are being enjoyed to the full, a deepening relationship with God can be maintained and genuine service for God can still be exercised. The second, the permissive, I reject on the grounds that it is irresponsible rather than loving, humanist rather than biblical, and self-centred rather than God-centred. And self-pleasing is of the essence of worldliness. Neither the prohibitionist nor the permissive view accurately reflects the Bible's teaching about interpersonal relationships.

. . . and self-centredness, self pleasing is of the essence of worldliness.

PRINCIPLE

The alternative

So the next question is: What *does* the Bible teach about relationships? Does it offer an alternative to the world's view? Does it help us to find a way between the two 'Christian views' caricatured above?

The Bible does not mention contemporary boy-girl relationships specifically. When the Bible was written, marriages were always arranged marriages. A young man's parents would find a suitable partner for him and make all the plans for the wedding.

The process of falling in love, as we understand it, did not apply. Therefore the authors who contributed to the Bible had no need to address themselves to this problem. But what the Bible does furnish us with is certain guidelines which apply to all the relationships we make. One of these comes in the challenge given by Jesus

> Love each other as I have loved you.

himself: 'Love each other as I have loved you'
(John 15:12).

How did Jesus love people?

He shared. Friendship, for Jesus, included complete openness and self-disclosure. Indeed, from John 15:15, it is possible to see that friendship is making everything known to your friend. It is sharing. It is telling your friend everything the Father has revealed to you. It includes emotional closeness, being in tune with your friend; intellectual closeness, enjoying the world of ideas; and spiritual closeness, delighting in the Father's love together.

He sacrificed. One of the stunning qualities of real friendship is self-sacrifice. In Jesus' terms, complete self-giving is what friendship is. A friend is someone who lays down his life for us, and for whom we lay down our lives. In true friendship there can be no holding back. This is why the element of choice is vital and pressing. We cannot love everyone in this costly way.

He chose. Friendship, for Jesus, did not happen by chance. He *chose* his friends *(John 15:16)*. He did not open himself, in the self-revealing way I have described, to everyone. Neither did he reveal his innermost secrets to all those who would be befriended by him. He was careful and selective. Wise. From the twelve, he selected three friends with whom he would enjoy most intimacy and from that threesome emerged one: John 'the beloved'.

He was concerned. Jesus' concern for his friends knew no limits. He was concerned for their physical well-being, their emotional security and supremely for their spiritual welfare. His deepest expressed desire and burden was that his friends should remain true to God their Father *(John 17: 11-12)*.

He took responsibility. Jesus accepted full responsibility for those to whom he was close. Even so, friendship with Jesus was never a claustrophobic, exclusive or possessive affair. Far from being jealous if his friends showered affection on one another, Jesus actively encouraged this mutual free-flowing love (*John 15:16*). As one author expresses it: 'There is no greater love than the friendship of which Jesus speaks. The effects of this kind of relationship: the deepest and most intimate union imaginable'.

Donald Goergen,
The Sexual Celibate,
Seabury Press, 1974.

He drew out their potential. Jesus called Peter 'Rock' even though he was still immature and impetuous (*John 1:42*). He saw Peter's potential and encouraged his strengths.

The challenge confronting the Christian young person is to emulate Jesus in everything — including the forging of friendships with people of both sexes. It would seem, then, that there is an alternative to the world's view and to the prohibition and permissive theories. Christian young people can learn to make radical, responsible relationships which have a value all their own, in and of themselves.

How did Jesus love people?

He shared;
Friendship, for Jesus, included complete openness and self-disclosure.
He chose;
Friendship for Jesus did not happen by chance. He chose his friends.
He sacrificed;
One of the stunning qualities of real friendship is self-sacrifice.
He was concerned;
Jesus' concern for his friends knew no limits.
He took responsibility;
Jesus accepted full responsibility for those close to him.
He drew out their potential;
He saw Peter's potential and encouraged his strengths.

An alternative: learn to make radical responsible relationships which have a value in and of themselves.

17

Sift your motives: why am I wanting this relationship?

How can Jesus' principles apply to our relationships?

We have seen that real friendship, if we take Jesus as our example, never prevents our friend's growth, stifles his God-given ambition, or blocks his path to a fruitful ministry. Rather, it involves standing with him, helping him discover his gifts and his calling and then offering encouragement, prayer and support: 'You can do it.' The question we now face is: How can these principles be applied to boy-girl relationships?

1. Refuse to conform to peer and parental pressure to pair off. Even consider avoiding forming exclusive friendships at certain times in your career so that you are free to concentrate fully on your work or on a particular piece of ministry for God.

2. Don't go out with someone just because you have 'fallen in love' with him or her — just because your heart misses a beat or you go weak at the knees when you see that person.

3. Don't let looks or lust determine who you go out with.

4. Think and pray. Weigh carefully before God the implications of investing yourself in this particular relationship. Jesus did not choose his friends in the wake of a surge of emotion or because a person happened to be endowed with a good figure or fine features. He engaged his mind in every decision he made and always submitted these decisions to his Father, seeking his approval before he acted. Sift your motives with care, asking: Why am I wanting this relationship? Is it for my benefit or the other person's or both?

5. Resolve, in every friendship you make, to do all in your power to bring God's *shalom* (wholeness) to the person you befriend even though this will involve you in a consistent sacrificial giving of yourself.

6. Refuse to do anything which would cause

that person harm – mentally, spiritually or emotionally.

7. Be concerned for your friend's physical and emotional well-being.

8. Be concerned that he or she continues to grow spiritually.

9. Do all in your power to ensure that he or she continues to serve God faithfully.

10. Do all in your power to draw out the person's full potential.

So, should Christians pair off?

When two people apply these criteria to their relationship, both partners will benefit from the friendship even though they may never marry.

Such one-to-one friendships can give to both partners the emotional intimacy every young person yearns for: the kind of understanding and tender loving care which you used to enjoy from your parents when you were young (if the parent-child relationship was good); and which, one day, you will enjoy with your husband or wife if God entrusts you with the vocation of marriage and if that relationship is as rich as God intends it to be. Moreover, these relationships can be the apprenticeships of love, in the sense that young people learn how to give warmth to a person of the opposite sex and to receive love from him or her. I believe it takes a male to draw out the full femininity of a female and a female to draw out the full masculinity of a male and therefore such friendships can promote the growth of both partners.

Yes!

So the answer is 'Yes, but'. Yes, Christians may pair off.

But!

We must apply the standards Jesus set and resist the viewpoint of our sex-mad society which claims that pairing off is for sex.

chapter two

The petting problem

'Why is it wrong to have sex before marriage?'

'How far should Christians go if they don't agree with sex before marriage?'

'Surely with the contraceptives that are available, Christians should enjoy sex, which, after all, is only an extension of one person's love for another?'

'How far can we go? — obviously not the whole way, but when's far enough?'

'Surely having sex with each other would be a way of saying, "You're the only one for me and I love you most of all in this world." That can't be wrong! I know the Bible says that you should wait until you are married to have sex, but when the Bible was written times were different; you were either single or married. Now we have the option of going steady or living with someone, so I don't think we should interpret the Bible too strictly on this matter.'

Should Christians pair off? Yes, but . . . That was the conclusion we reached in chapter one. One big 'but' is this: But what about the problem of touch? What are couples supposed to do with the touch bomb? How do they resolve the petting problem? Is it right for two people who really love each other to sleep together? If not, where should we draw the petting line? And how on earth do you cool the sex urge? These are the kinds of questions many sincere, Bible-believing Christians are asking — like the girl who wrote to me on one occasion:

'I am eighteen and became a Christian six months ago. I have been going out with my boyfriend for over a year and we make love together. I've never really thought about it being wrong or right until just recently and it's causing me a lot of problems.

'On one side I've got parents who forbid it. On the other side I've got friends who think it's perfectly acceptable. Then I've got God telling us it's wrong, and I really can't understand why it's wrong. Of course, I understand why it's wrong for some people, but my boyfriend and I have such a great relationship. It's very hard for my boyfriend suddenly to hear from me that we can no longer have that side of a relationship. Surely

PROBLEM

BBC programme, July 1963

> **It seems that the chief concern of the world is to fan the flames with little thought for the consequences.**

Sunday Telegraph, 24 February 1985

there's room in the Christian faith to make your own decisions about things? Anyway, I find I'm rebelling against God because I just don't understand some of the Christian principles. It's important for me to be clear about my faith. I would be so grateful if you could write back to me.'

The world's view

As we began to see in chapter one, the world seems to be convinced that sex outside of marriage is permissible. This view was once summed up by Dr Alex Comfort, Nuffield Research Fellow in the Department of Zoology at University College, London:

'Chastity is no more a virtue than malnutrition.'

Films and television

The secular media supports this view. Take the film *Endless Love* for example. This is a powerful portrayal of the obsession of a sixteen-year-old boy for a fifteen-year-old girl. When challenged about the message the film communicates, Zefferelli, the producer, claimed: 'I'm not encouraging fifteen-year-olds to make love. They do that anyway. I'm just telling them it's quite normal.'

Again, the world's pressures begin very early.

The world is not concerned in the least to cool the sex urge. It seems that its chief concern is to fan the flames with little thought for the consequences. So once again it is relevant to hear what its voice is saying. It is against this background that the Christians who want to follow their Master's way are attempting to handle their passions.

Many teenagers watch blue videos and are influenced by them. As one teenager put it: 'I've seen at least half a dozen of these films. They show you all the different positions. You see something that looks good so you go and try it out.'

Soap operas, *Dallas, Dynasty* and the rest, convey the same basic message: sex is normal, healthy. Couples are jumping in and out of bed with each other and sex is equated with money, power and social status. A genuine relationship, if it is mentioned at all, seems of secondary importance. The result is that many impressionable young people imbibe the message: promiscuity is the healthy norm.

'The single most powerful sexual stimulant in existence is the film; its seductive lure is almost overwhelming. It is difficult to imagine that any young person who watches today's films regularly could ever again feel — let alone think — about sexual intercourse in the same way that his parents did.'

Lewis Smedes, *Sex in the Real World*, Lion, 1976, p. 103

Pop culture

Pop songs reinforce the belief that premarital sex is the norm. In recent years a stream of popular records which openly make this assumption has been released. Most notable perhaps are George Michael's 'I Want your Sex' (CBS Records, 1987) and Frankie Goes to Hollywood's orgasmic single 'Relax'. 'Relax' became a cult record and held the number one chart slot for several weeks despite being banned by the BBC.

Relax don't do it
When you want to go to it
Relax don't do it
When you want to come . . .

Island Records ZZT, 1984

Peer pressure

We are so bombarded with such lyrics that it is impossible to tune them out of our minds. They assault us as we shop, as we travel and every time we switch on the radio.

But even harder to resist is the personal influence exerted by our peer group, especially if our friends are not Christians or if those close to us have not recognized the subtle power of pop culture.

Celia Haddon puts it well in the introduction to her book *The Limits of Sex*. 'Since sex is a sign of health, the new orthodoxy expects all of us to

PROBLEM

be practising it. People feel ashamed if they live without sex, and nowadays even Catholic priests are sometimes wondering if celibacy is perhaps a mistake.

As for young people, they feel the pressure to conform, this time towards sexual practice rather than virginity. 'I'm a shy girl and have led a sheltered life,' wrote a correspondent in the British teenage magazine, *Honey*. 'By the time they were sixteen, most of my friends said they'd lost their virginity and I began to feel like a freak. I agreed to make love to my boyfriend just to be a normal girl like everyone else.'

Parent power

For some Christians problems arise, as we have seen, from parents who, fearing religious fanaticism, urge their offspring to be normal; to sleep with their partner.

Pressure from 'the experts'

As with pairing off, so with genital sex, the world also bombards young people with the views and opinions of 'experts'. These people appear on radio and television and the guidelines they give are accepted as society's new morality. For example, Dr Miriam Stoppard, author and influential television personality, has written a book for young teenagers with the aim of enabling them to make 'responsible and informed judgements' about relationships which include genital sex. In her book *Talking Sex* she describes the feelings many young people say they enjoy after they have indulged in premarital intercourse:

'The loss of virginity has an enormous effect on boys . . . boys have mainly positive feelings. You feel you have matured, you're proud of yourself and feel a sense of accomplishment. You feel like a man and it's something you can boast about. You feel you've conquered something, and are relieved that you can finally tell the truth if someone asks you if you're still a virgin.'

'Experts' appear on radio and television and the guidelines they give are accepted as society's new morality.

Scripture on sex

Sex is a gift from God

God is pro-sex. You will find nothing negative in the Bible about the act of sexual intercourse. On the contrary. Key passages from the Old and New Testaments show how highly sex is thought of.

Take *Genesis 2:18-25* as a starting-point. Here God deliberately and intentionally creates for man a companion with a separate sexual identity, which the man finds attractive and magnetic. Different. God creates their differences, not for separateness, but for oneness. God intended that the two should be reunited so that the needs created by their deep loneliness would be met in each other. This fellowship and 'unity' included all levels of intimacy including the genital. *Genesis 2:25* is an appreciation of the human body: 'The man and the woman were both naked, but they were not embarrassed' (*Good News Bible*). It was even more positive than that. They celebrated. They delighted in each other, physically and emotionally and in the presence of God. And God saw that it was good.

And look at the Song of Solomon. If ever extravagant language was used to describe sensuous love-play it is used in this book of the Bible. As in Genesis, the language used is celebratory. God does not have a down on sex; he created men and women genitally equipped to lead one another into 'transports of delight'. In the context of committed marital love, this is the pleasure he wants them to give to one another.

The New Testament takes up this joyful theme. When Jesus is asked questions concerning marriage and sex, he reminds his hearers of the basic principles outlined in Genesis: sex and marriage are God's gifts, planted in Paradise. 'Haven't you read the

PRINCIPLE

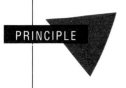

scripture . . . in the beginning the Creator made people male and female? And God said, ". . . the two will become one" ' (*Matthew 19:4-6, Good News Bible*). In other words, 'Don't you understand that from the beginning God intended that men and women should be attracted to each other; they should satisfy one another?' And Paul, who is often accused of being negative about sex, underlines the God-givenness of marital union. In *Ephesians 5* he initiates an amazing analogy. Marital oneness which includes the sexual union is not unlike the relationship which exists between Christ, the bridegroom, and his bride, the church: close, permanent, binding. No-one can find a higher, more wholesome picture of the love of man and woman than that.

So God is pro-sex. Indeed, sex is God's gift. But notice that it seems to have one context only: *marriage*.

Biblical straight talking

Adultery and casual sex are forbidden. Just as sex within marriage is praised, celebrated and applauded, so sex outside of marriage is condemned. The Bible uses two words for extra-marital sex: adultery and fornication, or sexual immorality, to use the more modern translation.

By adultery the Bible means sexual intercourse between a married person and someone to whom that person is not married. Of adultery, the Bible has this to say:

Exodus 20:14 — 'You shall not commit adultery.'
Deuteronomy 5:18 — 'You shall not commit adultery.'
Matthew 19:18 — 'You shall not commit adultery.'
Romans 13:9 — 'You shall not commit adultery.'

The message could not be clearer if it flashed on our bedroom wall in neon lights. Do not indulge in sexual intercourse with a person who is married to someone else.

The biblical writers are equally agreed about casual sex: sexual immorality or 'fornication'. Fornication means genital intercourse with someone to whom you are not married. The Bible insists that this kind of behaviour is not permissible for one who calls himself a Christian.

1 Corinthians 6:13 — 'The body is not meant for sexual immorality, but for the Lord.'

1 Corinthians 6:18 — 'Flee from sexual immorality.'

Colossians 3:5 — 'Put to death ... sexual immorality, impurity, lust, evil desires.'

1 Thessalonians 4:3 — 'Avoid sexual immorality.'

Paul's advice, 'Flee immorality', has echoes of *Genesis 39:12* about it. There we hear Potiphar's wife pleading with Joseph: 'Come to bed with me!' But Joseph refuses. Over and over again: 'My master has withheld nothing from me except you, because you are his wife. How then could I do such a wicked thing and sin against God?' (*39:9*).

Day after day Potiphar's wife persisted. And day after day Joseph refused. Until one day she caught him by the cloak as she made her familiar plea: 'Come to bed with me!' But leaving his cloak in her hand, Joseph 'ran out of the house.'

From this I conclude that both Paul and the writer of Genesis would persuade us that it is better to lose our coat than our virginity outside marriage.

Why the embargo?

1. Intercourse conveys the message 'You are special to me.' This involves marriage.

2. Marriage means a permanent, public commitment to each other in God's plan.

3. God does not want to expose his children to unnecessary harm.

> **God's gift of sex has one context only: Marriage.**

Some clear reasons

If it is so wonderful, why is sex to be limited to marriage? Is God a divine spoilsport? Did he provide this delight only to say, 'Yes, but you can't have it, you're not old enough, you're not married'? Why is the context for sexual intercourse marriage and marriage only?

PRINCIPLE

From a vast variety of reasons, I propose to consider three.

First, we must ask ourselves what genital intercourse really is. For too long the myth has been spread abroad that sexual intercourse means simply release of tension, ejaculation of sperm, the contentment of the orgasmic experience. Sexual intercourse does include all this, but also much more. Far from being an animalized act, it is also a language capable of conveying profound messages, albeit non-verbally. Within the context of marriage, it conveys the soothing message, 'You are uniquely special to me.' Within the context of marriage, it conveys the healing message, 'I find my place of belonging, my reason for being, in you.' Within the context of marriage, it is the language of permanent, unending, faithful love which alone can eliminate the fear of rejection and the pain of abandonment.

Second, we must consider what the ideal of marriage is. Marriage, as God planned it, means commitment, permanence, fidelity. It means tenderness, understanding, the cluster of intimacies we looked at in chapter one.

Put these two superlatives together: a superlative, non-verbal language of love (non-verbal because it transcends the world of words), and a superlative, uniting relationship, and you begin to understand the metaphor Paul uses when he reminds us that the genital union was intended, by the divine architect, to reflect the depth of the oneness and the degree of the commitment and the mystery of the relationship which have always existed between God the Father and God the Son. Genital fusion in any context other than marriage can never even begin to reflect this wonder, this mystery, this other-worldliness. In any other context it is therefore second best, and God does not want his children either to taste the bitter dregs of the second best or to be content with this substitute for the real thing.

Nor does God want to expose his children to unnecessary harm. That is the third reason why he exhorts us to keep sexual intercourse for

marriage. Here are four of the risks we run if we abandon God's plan:

1. The pain of abandonment

Genital intercourse, as I have said, is the non-verbal language God created for married couples to communicate that consoling message: 'You are unique, special.'

Remove the act from the context of permanence and you have that most deeply disturbing of all emotions: the pain of abandonment.

If you have ever seen a rag doll lying on the garden lawn, dirty, soggy from rain or dew, and soiled, and if you have ever wondered how it might feel to be such a discarded toy, you are very near an accurate identification with the feeling of abandonment which sweeps over people who have allowed, or been forced to allow, their bodies to be used by another under the pseudonym of 'love' and who have then been relegated to the proverbial scrap heap.

I encounter the anguish such people experience time and again in my counselling work. I think

> **. . . to have been used, then tossed aside is devastating.**

29

of the girl who told me she had had intercourse with her boyfriend because she thought he felt about her the same depth of love she felt for him. The day after they had slept together he admitted: 'There's nothing in it as far as I'm concerned. I just know where to touch a girl to make her sexually excited.'

To have been used, then tossed aside, is devastating. It drives people to drink, to drugs, to suicide, in an attempt to block out the pain which refuses to go away. And God, far from being a spoilsport, wants to protect us from this kind of pain.

And men are not exempt from the pain: 'After Ruth told me she didn't love me any more, I was stunned. I remember walking and walking round the park, trying to make sense of it all. The hurt inside seemed more than I could take.'

2. Pregnancy

There is always the possibility that the girl will conceive a child. No contraceptive device is foolproof. Newspapers spell out horrifying stories of unwanted pregnancies, tugs of love, even of young mothers murdering their unwanted babies.

In Christian circles too, as counsellors, we are asked to help young women who have suffered the indignity and trauma of back-street or legal abortion as well as those whose babies (conceived out of wedlock) have miscarried or had to be adopted. In all of these situations the pain and shame, not only of the couple concerned, but of the relatives and the fellowship to which they belong, are indescribable. No wonder God wants to protect us.

3. VD

The already high incidence of VD increases yearly. Contrary to beliefs once common, VD cannot be contracted from toilet seats or swimming pools, soiled towels or dirty sheets; it can be contracted only through sexual involvement with someone who is already carrying the disease.

Venereal disease is serious. Gonorrhoea, the

disease which is ever on the increase, produces a severe inflammation of the sex organs, and unless it is treated early and effectively, can leave the genitals scarred and distorted and can even lead to life-long sterility. Syphilis is even more deadly. If left untreated, it produces unsightly scabs on the body, can result in the malformation of limbs, and can be passed on to children at birth.

And recent research has shown that sexually transmitted disease is the commonest cause of arthritis in young people. It is believed that such disease is responsible for as many as 10,000 new cases a year in Britain alone.

In addition to the dangers of contracting VD, we must consider the danger of cancer of the cervix. Medical research over the past few years has shown that cancer of the neck of the womb (the cervix) is far more common among girls who have indulged in genital intercourse with several partners than in those who have abstained. It is believed that the neck of the womb during the teenage years is highly sensitive, and exposure to semen, particularly if the semen is from a variety of partners, increases the likelihood of a cancerous condition developing. It follows that teenage girls who sleep around automatically place themselves at risk: the risk of developing cancer.

God wants to protect us from this wastage of life, from these debilitating diseases. The answer is not to use the sheath but to keep genital intercourse within the context God has ordained: the committed relationship of marriage.

God wants to protect us from this wastage of life.

4. AIDS

If VD as defined above is a problem, how much more is the spread of AIDS? The subject has been so well canvassed that little more needs to be said here except to emphasize that as I write, recent figures have highlighted the fact that heterosexuals are as much at risk of catching the AIDS virus as homosexuals. According to an article in the *Observer* in August 1987, over 2,000 heterosexuals in Britain have already caught the virus through sexual activity, and these figures increase the fear

PRINCIPLE

Observer, 23 August 1987:
'Epidemic feared as AIDS
affects 2,000 heterosexuals'

that an epidemic will break out among heterosexuals in due course. As Dr Andrew Moss, an AIDS epidemiologist, put it: 'All heterosexual studies point in the same direction: that sexual partners of people infected have a chance of between 15 and 50 per cent of contracting the virus through vaginal sex.'

AIDS victim's diary of death

This is the last testament of AIDS victim Douglas Lambert, a British television actor who agreed to keep a diary after he learned he was dying of the disease.

'I'm wasting away, but I just can't eat. I'm about to have half a grapefruit which I seem to like and seem to have a lot of.

I had my little cry today. I have a little cry every day now I think — just a little one.

Nov. 14. I was just so incredibly sick all day.

Nov. 18. I was on television last night. I was too sick to go so they called me and I did an interview via telephone.

After I did the show I was just lying around and

I proceeded to get very sick again, so it was another unpleasant night.

Nov. 22. My body has aged 30 years in three months. It must be one of the majors of AIDS that it all of a sudden hits and it hits hard, and the end of your life is just there.

Nov. 29. Help people. It is the loneliest disease on earth. Even with people around you it's lonely, and to be truly alone, feeling this way, is everything you've feared your whole life . . . I'm a young man but everything has speeded up to the point where I'm also rather old. My body is old. My mind is probably old now, too . . . It's very strange because I wasn't ready to become old.

Oh, please, if you know anyone with this dreadful disease, be kind, be gentle, be generous because whatever your fears may be their pain and suffering is much greater. And they're vulnerable.
Dec. 2. My days are miserable now. The sickness is spacing me out more and more.
Dec. 4. I am now waiting for morphine. I don't want to become a vegetable.
Dec. 10. The doctor has put me on morphine because I was in such discomfort and er . . .'

These were the last words recorded by Douglas Lambert. He died at his London home six days later on December 16, 1986.

Daily Telegraph, Australia, Saturday, 4 April, 1987.

God is not a spoilsport. Love is what God is: protective, discerning, all-wise love. That is why genital intercourse, according to the Bible's teaching, knows of only one context: marriage.

How far can we go?

PRACTICE

Clearly, sexual intercourse is 'out'. But what about petting? Or holding hands? Where do we draw the line? The Bible does not address itself to these specific questions. But it does give clear principles. One is: 'Love your neighbour as yourself.'

Another is: 'Love one another as I have loved you.'

We must use our human reason as we work out what that means. Four key questions help us to do this: Is this practice dangerous in any way? Is it truly loving? How does it affect us spiritually? Is it natural?

It is also worth asking some other pertinent questions: 'Is my chief concern to live biblically or am I wanting to squeeze as much sexual licence as I possibly can out of a holy God? What are my motives for wanting a sexual relationship?'

I realize that you cannot really draw an accurate slide-rule or ladder of physical contact; that a warm hug on one occasion may be less erotic than the touch of a hand on another. But I believe a visual aid might help our discussion even though it is an inadequate or, in some sense, an inaccurate one.

It might look something like this:

Scale of touch

Genital intercourse

Oral sex

Mutual masturbation

Heavy petting

Petting

Prolonged kissing

Kissing

Cuddling

Embracing

Holding hands

We have already observed that the Bible's teaching on the context of sexual intercourse implies that Bible-observing Christians will draw the line below genital intercourse. That is, they will exclude it from their pre-marital experience. The scale will therefore look like this

Scale of touch

Genital intercourse

Oral sex

Mutual masturbation

Heavy petting

Petting

Prolonged kissing

Kissing

Cuddling

Embracing

Holding hands

PRACTICE

Thus far the position is clear, though perhaps not welcome to those who wish the Bible was not so definite. But what about the rest of the scale?

Oral sex

Technically, oral sex is not full intercourse. Even though both partners may be brought to a climax, virginity is not lost. Is it then permissible or not? Think it through for yourself by applying some of the questions on page 34:

1. Is this practice dangerous? It can be. Gonorrhoea of the throat may be contracted in this way. Statistics suggest that it often is. In oral sex the girl admits her boyfriend's penis into her mouth and caresses it with her lips and tongue and the male stimulates his girlfriend's clitoris with his mouth and tongue. If the mucous membrane in the mouth comes into contact with a diseased sex organ, then gonorrhoea of the throat may develop. Some medical researchers also believe that a person with a cold sore on the lip who indulges in oral-genital sex may be responsible for transmitting venereal disease. And, according to Dr Adrian Mindel, consultant in genito-urinary medicine at London's Middlesex Hospital, at least a third of the nation's genital herpes sufferers (there are 20,000 new cases every year) contract the disease through oral sex.

Oral sex has been described as 'the sex fad of the seventies'. Popularized by glossy magazines, sex books, blue movies and so-called art, the craze continues. As Dr Miriam Stoppard discovered back in 1982 when writing her book *Talking Sex,* 'quite a few of you have experienced some kind of oral sex by the time you're sixteen.' And, as a survey in *Buzz* magazine in 1986 showed, Christians under twenty-five frequently resort to this kind of sexual intimacy outside of marriage. But we need to apply our second question.

> Is my chief concern to live biblically or to squeeze in as much sexual licence as I can?

2. Is it loving? Love involves taking responsibility for the loved one; not inflicting unnecessary harm on them. But many girls endure rather than enjoy oral sex. Some find it quite nauseating.

3. Does it affect our spiritual life? Many people have found themselves plagued by guilt after they have indulged in such intimacies. 'Twenty-one-year-old Genette recalls her fiancé demanding oral sex with her. "It finally proved to me he didn't really love me," she said. "And it made me certain that I didn't want to marry him. We split up shortly afterwards." '

20th Century Sex, Word Books, 1987, p. 43

Mutual masturbation to orgasm

It often happens that two people who love each other agree to abstain from full genital intercourse, but, while withholding the final act, the penetration of the vagina by the penis, they stimulate one another's sex organs with the hands until each partner is brought to full orgasmic experience. Again, technically, intercourse has not taken place and the question is often asked: 'Is this practice permissible or deceitful?'

Again, apply some of the test questions and think the thing through for yourself. Is it dangerous? Again, it can be because it is possible to conceive a child in this way. Even though full intercourse has not taken place enough sperm may be spilt into the entrance of the vagina to fertilize the female egg. (See Joyce Huggett, *Growing into Love*, IVP, 1982, p. 87.) Is it loving? Think of the possible repercussions of this practice. It sometimes happens that a woman grows so accustomed to manual manipulation of this kind that adjustment to full intercourse after marriage proves difficult. This sometimes even results in frigidity.

Is this therefore responsible loving? Or do you, perhaps, need to push the boundary back a notch?

Scale of touch

3

Genital intercourse

Oral sex

Mutual masturbation

Heavy petting

Petting

Prolonged kissing

Kissing

Cuddling

Embracing

Holding hands

Heavy petting

By heavy petting I mean the practice of slipping your hands inside a girl's dress to fondle her breasts; or undoing the zip of your boyfriend's trousers to fondle his genitals; or stroking your girlfriend's thighs or genitalia. Heavy petting includes lying together in a state of undress from the waist upwards, or fully naked; lying side by side or on top of one another.

This kind of petting may be enormously exciting at first, but of course, it makes us demand more. We need to acknowledge the cold clinical fact that there is something about naked flesh which brings to the surface the full force of sexual desire. As one girl described it to her boyfriend when his hands started wandering down her body: 'There's a tigress living inside me, and if you touch me there it will leap out at us.' She was right.

There's a tigress living inside me, and if you touch me there it will leap out at us.

That tiger has to be tamed; not chained, nor mounted and ridden, but trained. Tiger-training becomes much more difficult with every new and exciting form of touch. That is why you may have to bring the boundaries back another notch:

Scale of touch

Genital intercourse

Oral sex

Mutual masturbation

Heavy petting

Petting

Prolonged kissing

Kissing

Cuddling

Embracing

Holding hands

Petting

By petting I mean fondling one another's breasts and genitals outside the clothes. I also mean any form of lying together. Included in petting comes prolonged kissing: any kiss which is more than a leisurely peck and particularly any kiss which involves that highly sensitive organ, the tongue.

What we have to recognize is that any form of petting is dynamite. As one young friend of mine admitted after kissing his girlfriend for the first time: 'It was fantastic. But it was frightening too. It brought to the surface such powerful feelings in me that I didn't even know were there. I know I'm going to have to cool it or I will lose control.' This young man brought the boundaries back two more notches.

PRACTICE

Scale of touch

5

Genital intercourse

Oral sex

Mutual masturbation

Heavy petting

Petting

Prolonged kissing

Kissing

Cuddling

Embracing

Holding hands

And by kissing, he meant a peck on the cheek! He could not trust himself to indulge in anything more intense for the time being.

'When's far enough?' That was one of the questions we started with. Different people will reach different answers to that question. But pay attention to the advice of older, wiser Christians. In April 1986, *Buzz* magazine commissioned a nationwide survey on Christians' attitudes to sex (later published as the book *20th Century Sex*). Over 2,000 readers returned a full and frank questionnaire. A fifth of these were married. Asked what advice these Christian married couples would give to courting couples, nine couples out of ten said:

Don't have intercourse before marriage.

Don't get involved in heavy petting either.

In many ways these marrieds seem to have been preaching to the converted. 99% of single Christians admitted that they wanted to wait until marriage for sex and two thirds also wanted to save heavy petting until their wedding night. Suddenly, it seems 'No' has become a fashionable word.

chapter three

Cooling the sex urge

'What situations are best to avoid if you don't want to go too far with your boyfriend/girlfriend by getting carried away?'

'When the flame of passion begins to burn, how do you quench it? Where is the fire extinguisher?'

'What I'd like to know is *how* — how do you channel your sexuality into forging warm friendships?'

'I'm a good-looking bloke who has never slept with anyone and as a student I'm finding it increasingly difficult to resist temptation. I'm the only one in my circle of friends who thinks sex before marriage is wrong.'

Quoted in *20th Century Sex*, p. 145

'Whenever a man and woman relate to each other as persons it adds an indefinable tinge of adventure and excitement, uncertainty and curiosity to the relationship. We should be conscious of it, accept it and rejoice in it. The more we affirm it with thanks, the less likely we are to be deluded by the fear that any sexually exciting relationship will lead to the bedroom.'

Lewis Smedes, *Sex in the Real World*, p. 96

PROBLEM

Yet, boy-girl relationships often do lead to the bedroom, as we have already seen. Conscious of the power of the temptation and equally conscious that the context for sexual intercourse is marriage, most Christians clamour for an answer to the question: How do we cool it? The survey on '20th Century Sex', conducted by *Buzz* magazine, highlighted this fact. 2,335 people responded to

PROBLEM

the survey. Of these 40% were males and 60% females. Nearly everyone fell into the 16-29 age bracket and 98% of them said they were committed Christians. Asked about their views on sex before marriage, a resounding 99% admitted that they believed that sexual intercourse should be kept within the marriage relationship. Two out of three thought couples should only kiss before marriage. But when asked to compare this fine theory with their own practice, half of those who advocated 'kissing only' failed to stay within this boundary and went on to petting and even intercourse. One in six admitted that they had had premarital intercourse after they had become Christians. They were aware that this was wrong but seemed to be confused about the reasons why it was wrong.

The questionnaire asked where these young Christians turn for help with their sexual problems. Most found their main source of teaching and support from Christian magazines and books, but three times as many admitted that they turn to the secular media for help rather than to the local church.

The world says — Try it and see

This trend troubles me because, as we have already seen, the world's view of sexual morality stands in stark contrast to the Bible's view. For a Christian, looking for ways of relating well to the opposite sex while still exercising sexual restraint, the secular media are very often the worst place to look for advice. The world's view is largely 'excite it' not 'cool it'. Here are some examples. Typical of the humanist philosophy which has swept through Western society in the past twenty-five years is this viewpoint voiced by a woman whose own marriage had broken up, chiefly, she claims, through sexual problems:

'To expect the girl to go into marriage as a virgin is just folly. There is so much that can go wrong with the physical relationship that I have become quite clear in my mind that no girl should

Katharine Trevelyan, *Fool in Love,* quoted by David Phypers, *Christian Marriage in Crisis,* Marc Europe, 1985, pp. 67-68

allow herself to become engaged till she has lain with her man and found joy, peace and release in it.'

And typical of the advice a young Christian would be given if he or she turned to the secular media for help would be this quotation from a book on sex which was on display at family planning clinics as early as the 1970s:

'We no longer believe in telling the young what to do, but if we were asked for advice . . . would say something like this: "Make love if you both feel like it. But first make sure you are safe . . . Your only safe course . . . is to go to a clinic (FPA or Brook Advisory Centre) and get advice on contraception. Making love is normal, healthy and pleasurable, and a means of communicating delight between human beings. Providing you are sincere with each other, and safe, . . . do it with a clear conscience; and we hope you enjoy it."'

Michael Lloyd-Jones and Maurice Hill, *Sex Education — The Erroneous Zone,* quoted by Mary Whitehouse, *Whatever Happened to Sex?,* Hodder and Stoughton, 1977, p. 37

And from Sweden comes this advice: 'You may go to bed with someone for a variety of reasons: because you are infatuated, in love, curious, worried about being different, anxious to please your partner, afraid of losing him or her, or just plain randy. And intercourse can be satisfying on a purely sensual level, regardless of the depth of feeling involved, so long as both partners reach the desired climax. Moral attitudes are irrelevant as a basis for judging the reasons for going to bed, still less for condemning them.'

Bent Claesson, *Boy Girl — Man Woman,* quoted by Mary Whitehouse, *Whatever Happened to Sex?,* p. 96

More recently, a Health Education pamphlet on AIDS advises: 'The fewer sexual partners you have, the less risk you have of coming into contact with someone who has the virus . . . Using a condom (a sheath, or rubber), during sex will reduce the risk of getting the virus and other sexually transmitted diseases too.'

There is no mention of abstinence from premarital sex.

No wonder one twenty-one-year-old woman wrote to *Buzz* magazine: 'The pressure is always

'High Monogamy—
a feast available
only to those
who are willing
and able to engage
life on a deeply
personal level,
giving all, holding
back nothing.'

on me to give up my morals. The media is the worse for this.'

What do church leaders say?

Nine out of ten of the *Buzz* readers who responded to the sex survey felt that Christian leaders were failing to give adequate teaching on the vital subject of sex. 'Leaders disagree,' was the main reason given for this apparent lack.

'Or they can't explain their advice,' was another suggestion made. This leads to the kind of confusion Graham Turner tuned into when he interviewed students and others about their relationships:

'Not nearly so many of her friends had had sex,' said Helen, because of the way they'd been brought up. "Was that," I inquired, "because they were Christians?" "That's not fair!" she retorted. Christianity had nothing to do with it, because it didn't rule out sex before marriage. She knew a lot of girls who went to church who weren't virgins.

Emma agreed. "We've been given the power to love," she declared, "and we ought to use it." As Christians, they found it really hard to be stuck with non-trendy, boring labels like no-sex-before-marriage. At their church, they certainly didn't tell them it was wrong'.

Graham Turner, *Sunday Telegraph,* 24 February 1985

On the other hand, when the Australian government was about to launch its AIDS campaign, the *Catholic Leader,* widely read by Australian Roman Catholics, published a leading article: 'AIDS campaign: chastity the sure option.'

'Abstinence is the best way to beat AIDS. There is no doubt about that,' admitted Ms Ita Buttrose, head of the National Advisory Committee on AIDS. 'I am surprised that some people believe others are not capable of being chaste or faithful. Clearly, there are numbers who are not. Clearly, there are many who are.'

Catholic Leader, 29 March 1987

What does the Bible say?

Against this confused background, the Bible speaks clearly and incisively. It does not set out to answer the specific questions some Christians ask. You will nowhere find a verse which says, for example: 'You may kiss for six seconds but not for six minutes.' But what the Bible does give is guidelines — principles on which each Christian must build his or her behaviour patterns.

1. Live in obedience to Jesus

The first of these is: 'Live in obedience to Jesus.' This is a principle we must always keep before us — especially in today's spiritual climate. We live in an age when the church has discovered the joy and power of spontaneous worship. Quite rightly, we are encouraged to lose ourselves in wonder, love and praise. But the danger is that we begin to see our sovereign Lord only as a friend, only as a dancing partner in the ball of exuberant worship. We forget that he is the Master and Lord who addressed to his disciples the very solemn words recorded in *Luke 6:46:* 'Why do you call me "Lord, Lord," and do not do what I tell you?'

'There is joy in obedience' (*Amy Carmichael*).

We saw in chapter two what the Bible's clear instructions are:

'Avoid sexual immorality' (*Acts 15:20*).

'It is actually reported that there is sexual immorality among you . . . Shouldn't you have been filled with grief?' (*1 Corinthians 5:1-2*).

'Avoid sexual looseness like the plague!' (*1 Corinthians 6:18, J.B. Phillips' translation*).

'Obedience to God is the most infallible evidence of sincere and supreme love to him' (*Nathanael Emmons*).

2. Live in the presence of Jesus

It becomes easier to live in obedience to Jesus if we learn to live in his presence. The question to ask is not 'How would we behave if Jesus were here before us?' but 'How should we behave since Jesus is here before us?' In other words, we are

> **In today's spiritual climate we are quite rightly encouraged to lose ourselves in wonder. But the danger is that we begin to see our sovereign Lord only as a dancing partner in the ball of exuberant worship.**

47

Anthony Bloom, *Living Prayer,*
Libra, 1976, p. 12.

not playing 'let's pretend', but rather we are asking a question of real and immediate importance. The Lord is here. We are in the presence of the invisible Lord constantly.

'We must learn to behave in the presence of the invisible Lord as we would in the presence of the Lord made visible to us. This implies primarily an attitude of mind and then its reflection upon the body. If Christ were here, before us, and we stood completely transparent to his gaze, in mind as well as in body, we would feel reverence, the fear of God, adoration, or else perhaps terror, but we should not be so easy in our behaviour as we are.'

3. Bring the will into alignment with God's

What this means, of course, is that we bring our wills into alignment with Jesus' will. The key to victory lies in the will. When I pointed this out to a group of Christians on one occasion, the face of one of the girls brightened noticeably. Her eyes sparkled as the realization dawned on her: 'Yes, it is possible, isn't it? I mean, you can discipline yourself. It all depends on the will. Perhaps that's where the elusive off-switch hides — in the will.'

'We must be prepared to do God's will and pay the cost . . . We see that we cannot partake deeply of the life of God unless we change profoundly. It is therefore essential that we should go to God in order that he should transform and change us . . . But it is not a change of mind alone that we call conversion. We can change our minds and go no farther; what must follow is an act of will and unless our will comes into motion and is redirected godwards, there is no conversion; at most there is only an incipient, still dormant and inactive change in us.'

Anthony Bloom, *Living Prayer,*
pp. 64-66

With an act of the will, then, we must constantly bring our lives into alignment with the will of the Father, or, more accurately, ask God to bring our wills into alignment with his. Prayer must become the alignment centre. Prayer must be the place where we sweat out the fearsome battle Jesus fought in his temptation in the wilderness. Prayer must become the place where, like Jesus, we make our choice: to live a life centred around Number One, gratifying self no matter who gets hurt or deprived, or to deny ourselves the delights of self-gratification so that we fulfil the law of the King.

Aligning ourselves with Jesus cannot happen without a struggle. The tug to live selfishly, especially when sex is involved, is very strong. But it can be done by struggling, by co-operating with the Holy Spirit, and by opening ourselves to the comfort and presence of the love of God.

4. Seek God's transforming power

The love of God. That is also key to solving the problem. St Augustine used to say: 'I will work as though everything depended on me and I will pray as though everything depended on God.'

That is a good maxim. For the purposes of this book, perhaps we could rewrite it: 'I will discipline my will as though everything depended on me and I will seek an inner transformation from God's Spirit as though everything depended on him.' Victory lies in self-discipline and in the inner transformation which is a gift from God given by his Spirit. In particular, we need to ask God to cleanse us from hypocrisy and self-deceit and to cause the fruit of self-control to mature and ripen in us. Without these particular enablings we shall fall short of our own and God's standards very often — in thought, word and deed.

> **I will work as though everything depended on me and I will pray as though everything depended on God.'**

PRACTICE

Watching our thinking

And our thoughts are important, as Jesus reminds us with typical ruthlessness:

'You have heard that it was said to the people in the old days, "Thou shalt not commit adultery." But I say to you that every man who looks at a woman lustfully has already committed adultery with her — in his heart. Yes, if your right eye leads you astray pluck it out and throw it away;

49

PRACTICE

it is better for you to lose one of your members than that your whole body should be thrown on to the rubbish-heap' *(Matthew 5:27-29, J.B. Phillips' translation)*.

Or again, to quote Paul: 'Here is a last piece of advice. If you believe in goodness and if you value the approval of God, fix your minds on whatever is true and honourable and just and pure and lovely and praiseworthy . . . and you will find that the God of peace will be with you' *(Philippians 4:8-9, J.B. Phillips' translation)*.

Jesus said these things, not to make life hard for us, but to help us travel unscathed along this tortuous path of being healthily sexual and at the same time remaining spotless in his sight. Pictures of pin-ups, pornographic magazines, and blue movies and videos are created to encourage us to feast on the visual stimuli which Jesus warns will lead us into sin. If we are to be responsible and Christlike, therefore, we shall heed his warning, and though we may not go so far as to pluck our eyes out in a literal sense, we shall be sensible enough to put lustful literature on the rubbish heap.

How to control thought life

1. Remember the old saying: 'You can't stop the birds flying over your head but you can stop them nesting in your hair.' In other words, you may not be able to stop lustful thoughts coming into your mind but you can refuse them permission to take up residence there. Tip them out for the rubbish they are.

2. Bear in mind Paul's teaching: 'Whatever is true . . . whatever is pure, whatever is lovely, whatever is admirable . . . think about such things *(Philippians 4:8)*. Let this verse help you decide which videos and films and plays you spend time watching and which books and magazines you spend time reading. Fill your mind with things that are good. Shun what is shoddy and impure, acknowledging the power of visual stimuli.

3. Recognize at what time of day and where lustful thoughts most frequently plague you. Plan

> **Sexy clothes are not only unwise but unloving because they make self-control difficult for others.**

a strategy to combat them. If bedtime equals lustful fantasies, sit up in bed and write letters or read a novel instead of lying there indulging in fantasies. Or if certain posters or pictures arouse you unhelpfully, discipline yourself to avoid feasting on them.

4. Ask God to give you the mentality which can look at a pretty girl or an attractive man with appreciation but without lustful desires.

5. Open yourself to a touch of the grace of God who co-operates with us in our battle against sin and the devil.

6. Refuse to believe the lie of the Evil One who would try to persuade us that sexual thoughts and fantasies and an active sex life are necessary if we are to be fulfilled.

7. Remember that your body and mind are temples of the Holy Spirit, to be kept pure for God.

Leading ourselves out of temptation

We must be equally ruthless about our behaviour. For example, we must watch the way we dress. Provocative dress eggs people on. So we will avoid wearing jeans specially designed 'to make you sexy', perfume guaranteed to inflame the passion, see-through blouses which leave little to the imagination, or skin-tight T-shirts. Girls won't go bra-less. We will recognize that nakedness or near-nakedness and any form of undressing are in themselves powerful stimuli; such dress — or states of undress — are not only unwise but unloving because they make self-control difficult for one's partner and Christians in general.

And we will learn to be utterly practical — to recognize that certain parts of the body are highly sensitive, erogenous zones: breasts, nipples, thighs, genitals, even the ear lobes! If our partner's hands should stray on to these areas, we shall push them away, tenderly but firmly. As Walter Trobisch so sensibly said: 'A slap on the fingers can be a greater proof of love than a French kiss.' If our partner should push that hand away, we will show our respect by keeping the hand away.

Love is a Feeling to be Learned, IVP, 1974, p. 125

PRACTICE

Keeping in touch with others

Lovers love to be together, talking about their love, or just being with each other. But we will make sure that the majority of our time is not spent in a steamed-up car, a small bedsit or any other place where the physical side of the relationship is allowed to dominate. And we will make sure that both of us remain part of a group; a particular circle of friends, the music group, the youth group or whatever it is. The balance is difficult to keep, partly because time seems so short when the deliciousness of falling in love happens to you and

partly because possessiveness and jealousy set in so quickly; appropriate detachment is a difficult lesson to learn.

I sometimes find myself aching for couples where the girls act rather like the rhododendron roots I saw strangling some pine trees on one occasion. These girls cling to their boyfriends and refuse to let go. I agonize too, for the couples where a partner is consumed with jealousy every time the other enjoys the companionship of another member of the opposite sex. This afflicts men as well as women. One young man was honest

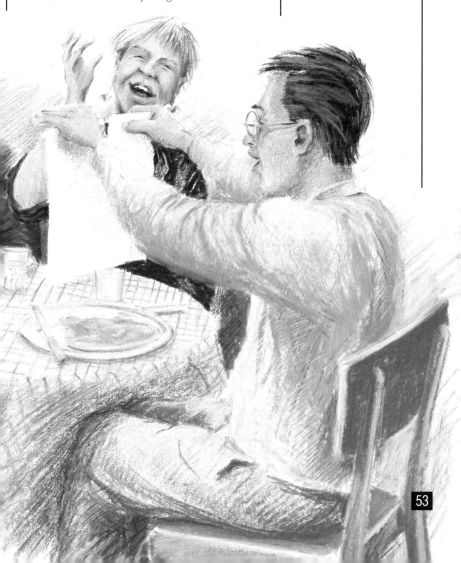

PRACTICE

enough to tell me how it felt:

'The jealousy inside me is terrible. It makes me want to possess her. I want her to walk with me to church. I want her to sit next to me. I want us to do everything together; little things like washing and shopping; big things like studying.'

A relationship like this where jealousy and possessiveness prevail is based on selfishness and not on love. This kind of relationship inevitably becomes claustrophobic, and people suffering from claustrophobia panic and search for an escape route. The fear of suffocation is frightening. And such fear nearly always marks the beginning of the demise of the relationship.

Stewards of our sexuality

It pays, therefore, to learn how to become wise stewards of our sexuality. The clamour for genital intercourse is reduced when we determine to explore all the avenues our relationships open up: sport, music, Christian activities, reading, walking, and the sheer joy of sharing the world of ideas and philosophies. When we concentrate on these, we find that a thousand strong and colourful strands bind us to one another in a rich and satisfying relationship. We can therefore learn to live well within the boundaries of touch we have set ourselves and enjoy what Walter Trobisch describes as the joyful pain of waiting.

Resisting the fast-food culture

We have seen that we live in a sex-saturated society which ignores the value of giving, caring relationships and which concentrates instead on a series of sexual kicks. But there is no need to ride on the crest of this cultural wave. It is possible to swim against it, to enjoy the challenge and exhilaration of living biblically and to be satisfied emotionally. Even those who once welcomed and applauded the sexual revolution of the sixties are admitting this:

'Advocates of multiple sex have a saying: "Why should I be satisfied with a sandwich when there's a feast out there?" They ask this only because they

> **Our aim should be to generate the atmosphere where the loved one's further growth can most easily take place.**

have never experienced High Monogamy. Those of us who have tried both tend to see it differently. Casual recreational sex is hardly a feast — not even a good, hearty sandwich. It is a diet of fast food served in plastic containers. Life's feast is available only to those who are willing and able to engage life on a deeply personal level, giving all, holding back nothing.'

George Leonard, 'Sex Without Love: Is It Enough?' *Woman's Journal,* March 1983

Remember the reason for boy-girl relationships

'Giving all, holding back nothing.' That, as we saw in chapter one, is love on the style of Jesus. This is vital to radical one-to-one relationships. They do not exist for self-gratification or sexual thrills, but to provide the environment where each friend can be loved into the next phase of personal growth.

Boy-girl relationships, as I see them, are the bridge which spans the gulf between parental love and marital love. Even though a particular friendship may never result in marriage, its main aim should be to generate the atmosphere where the loved one's further growth — emotional and spiritual — can most easily take place. If we keep this high purpose of radical relationships before us we need never regret any friendship but rather rejoice in the maturity God gave us through the one he entrusted to us to love — even for a short time.

Ten ways of ensuring that you don't go too far

1. Live in obedience to Jesus.

2. Live in the presence of Jesus.

3. Bring your will into alignment with God's.

4. Seek God's transforming power.

5. Watch your thought life.

6. Avoid tempting situations.

7. Keep in touch with others.

8. Be wise stewards of your sexuality.

9. Refuse to be conditioned by our culture.

10. Remember the real reason for radical relationships is to promote each other's growth.

chapter four

Is sexual sin the unforgivable sin?

PROBLEM

'I just can't forgive myself. And I can't forget. Is there any way of getting rid of the guilt sexual sin has left me with?'

'I know I've gone too far sexually with my boyfriend. Can God forgive me?'

'Can the stain of sexual sin ever be removed?'

'If I've failed in the past will it spoil the future?'

'Is it really possible for one's virginity to be restored?'

'I'm always making a mess of my life and blokes' lives by going too far physically. I don't understand what makes me do it when I know I'll regret it afterwards. What can I do about the guilt?'

'What happens if you've got hang-ups because you've been a victim of child abuse or rape?'

'Teenage abortions have soared to record levels in Nottingham .. The tally .... includes two abortions a week on Nottingham girls under 16, some as young as 12 and 13.'

That news item appeared in the *Nottingham Trader* in the summer of 1987. Two months later, the *Independent* painted an equally 'worrying' picture: 'A substantial proportion of Britain's most educated young people continue to be promiscuous.' This claim was made on the basis of the survey made by Dr Guy Cumbercatch and Dr Lorna Debney of Aston University, Birmingham. Of the 200 students who took part in the survey, 33% admitted to having had more than one sexual partner in the past year and 23% had had a one-night stand. 'In more than half of these casual relationships a condom was not used, although the students were well-informed about the risk of AIDS.'

Independent, 28 August 1987

Two years earlier, in 1985, a study was made of undergraduates at Liverpool University. This survey revealed that three out of five women reported that they had been abused sexually at some time, 31% before the age of fourteen. One in ten said they had suffered forced intercourse before the age of fourteen.

Christians are immune neither from being abused sexually nor from committing sexual sin.

I find this frightening because, as any Christian counsellor will testify, the guilt which is generated by such activity can be both crippling and long-lasting. That is why more Christians than I care to count have begged me for an answer to the question which plagues them: Is sexual sin forgivable?

The world's view

If you have read the first three chapters of this book, it will, by now, be obvious what the world would say in response to this question. To the unbeliever, it would be a non-question. Recreational sex, erotic films, pornographic literature and sexual fantasies are not viewed as sin. They are said to be fun. One of the leading protagonists for these activities is Richard Neville, editor of *Oz* magazine, who was prosecuted in London for his attempts to corrupt the young in *Children's Oz*. His testimony before the Longford Committee revealed that, in his opinion, certain of the more explicit magazines with their vivid descriptions of group sex and unusual sex techniques were 'liberating'.

'An orgy is an extremely healthy therapeutic activity,' he declared. 'Suppose you had a 15-year-old daughter, would you let her read such a magazine?' Mr Neville replied that certainly he would. 'Do you think this would encourage her to be promiscuous?' 'Certainly,' replied Mr Neville, 'that really is the whole point of such magazines . . .' He saw society being restructured in time so as to get rid of the hated nuclear family (mum, dad and the kids) which was with certain rare exceptions an inward-looking and on the whole self-destructive institution.'

> **Christians are immune neither from being abused sexually nor from committing sexual sin.**

Quoted in *Pornography: A Christian Critique* by John H. Court, IVP, USA, 1980, p. 124.

What does the Bible say?

Against this so-called 'liberated' background, we must now place the Bible's teaching on the subject of sex, sin and forgiveness.

The Bible acknowledges the problem:
Sex outside of marriage is a serious sin. It even

leaves an indelible stain:

'Flee from sexual immorality. All other sins a man commits are outside his body, but he who sins sexually sins against his own body' (*1 Corinthians 6:18*).

Sin separates us from God. 'The arm of the Lord is not too short to save, nor his ear too dull to hear. But your iniquities have separated you from your God; your sins have hidden his face from you, so that he will not hear' (*Isaiah 59:1-2*).

This is the bad news, and if the Bible left its teaching at that it would spell spiritual death for many of us. A couple once came to me in great despair because their relationship was being spoilt by self-indulgence. 'We know how far to go sexually. We know what is right. But we don't seem to be able to put this knowledge into practice. Why are we so undisciplined? Why doesn't God set us free from this powerful temptation?' But the Bible does not leave it at that. In a most moving story, it highlights the way Jesus dealt with a person who has sinned sexually:

Jesus went to the Mount of Olives. At dawn he appeared again in the temple courts, where all the people gathered around him, and he sat down to teach them. The teachers of the law and the Pharisees brought in a woman caught in adultery. They made her stand before the group and said to Jesus, 'Teacher, this woman was caught in the act of adultery. In the Law Moses commanded us to stone such women. Now what do you say?'

. . . Jesus bent down and started to write on the ground with his finger. When they kept on questioning him, he straightened up and said to them, 'If any one of you is without sin, let him be the first to throw a stone at her.' Again he stooped down and wrote on the ground.

At this, those who heard began to go away one at a time, the older ones first, until only Jesus was left, with the woman still standing there. Jesus straightened up and asked her, 'Woman, where are they? Has no-one condemned you?'

'No-one sir,' she said.

'Then neither do I condemn you,' Jesus declares. 'Go now and leave your life of sin.' (*John 8:1-11*)

Jesus' ministry to a promiscuous and adulterous generation was authoritative, powerful and full of compassion. This ministry had five parts to it.

1. He forgave.
2. He healed.
3. He released.
4. He re-established.
5. He challenged.

The Pharisees were demanding that the Jewish law should be honoured; that the woman should be stoned. But Jesus not only refuses to condemn ('Neither do I condemn you'), he protects her from the punishment which should have come to her — which is what forgiveness really involves. It was not that Jesus condoned her sin. He never does that. But he does love sinners. So much so that he cut this woman free from her failure, free from her guilt, free from her past so that she could be free to live a new and useful life. But he does not leave it at that. No. He challenges her to repent — that is, to live life differently; to give up her immoral way of life — to 'go now and leave your life of sin'.

Jesus' ministry to those who have 'failed'

One of the most exciting things that has been happening in the church in recent years is the rediscovery that Jesus is the same yesterday and today and for ever; that the ministry which set this woman free is still readily available from him for people who have sinned sexually. Let's look at the requirements.

1. Confess

I think of a girl who came to me admitting her failure. She had been committing heart-adultery

PRACTICE

by masturbating regularly while imagining that she was having intercourse with the man she was in love with.

'I wanted him so much. I wanted to feel his body enter mine. I wanted him to prove that he was the man of my dreams; the perfect lover. So instead of bringing my will into alignment with God's, I did what he has told us not to do, I gazed at my beloved lustfully and in my imagination he came to me and made love to me. It may only have been self-stimulation in physical reality but in my mind it was adultery. Yes. Adultery. In God's sight I am an adultress and his Word says so clearly that no adulterers will inherit the kingdom of God (*1 Corinthians 6:9*).'

This girl made a very simple confession to God in my presence:

'Oh, dear Lord, I recall with shame and anguish what I have done; how a part of me wants to be free and how another part of me wants to go on being lured by sin's dazzling lights. I do want to be free. Help me truly to be free by becoming inwardly free; free in the presence of temptation. You have given me the victory, Lord Jesus help me to take it and use it. So, tonight, I release him to you, and ask you to forgive and cleanse me.'

Nothing dramatic happened that night. She came into no feelings of release or euphoria. But she did sleep well. Next morning, when she woke up, she became acutely aware that God had heard and answered her prayer. This is what she wrote to God:

'Lord, thank you for that refreshing sleep. Thank you that I've woken up this morning sensing that a burden has been lifted. I'm free. Free from the past, free to love you and be loved again by you, free to serve you with energy again. Keep me pure. Help me to love with your pure, committed love, not with my own tarnished variety which only pollutes and distorts. Thank you for the refreshment your forgiveness brings.'

A few days later she admitted to me that her friendship with this young man was so much

deeper now that she had resolved to stop fantasizing in this sinful way. She was learning to love him because of who he was — a fine person striving to serve the living Lord — rather than because of the sexual kicks physical closeness might bring. She still found him attractive sexually, still found, from time to time, that thoughts of making love with him would spring up in her mind; but when the thoughts and desires came, she threw them out ruthlessly.

Such free forgiveness and strength of resolve is available to all those who know that their lives have been soiled and stained by sexual sin — whether of thought, word or deed. The words of John ring as true today as in the first century when he wrote them:

'If we freely admit that we have sinned, we find God utterly reliable and straightforward — he forgives our sins and makes us thoroughly clean from all that is evil . . . If we take up the attitude "we have not sinned," we flatly deny God's diagnosis of our condition and cut ourselves off from what he has to say to us' (*1 John 1:9, J. B. Phillips' translation*).

2. Receive God's forgiveness

Anyone suffering from the kind of guilt which gives rise to the question 'Is sexual sin the unforgivable sin?' will know that such guilt sometimes seems akin to torment. One girl recorded such feelings in her diary after she had committed a sexual sin whose memory threatened to plague her life:

'Father, I can only focus today on my unworthiness. I stand before you in rags and tatters — ashamed, stunned, bewildered. Could this be happening to me? Yes. It is happening to me. I stand before you ugly, impoverished and utterly bewildered. How could I grieve you so? How could I see those dazzling lights, turn from your love and pursue them?

'I feel so hurt, so bewildered, so angry, so

unhappy. I want to try to clear the rubble out of the way so that I can come to you to find and receive forgiveness, cleansing and peace but I don't know how to do it.

'I come to you this morning like a rolled-up, unforgivable ball. I can only cry, "Depart from me, for I am sinful, O Lord." I'm sorry, so sorry.'

Nine months later:

'I come to you shocked by this new reminder of the extent and longevity of my failure. I come to you with the dull ache of wounds and scars wide open. Can nothing heal this pain or shift this crushing load of guilt?

'You saw the devastating results of skating on thin ice. You see the broken fragments of me. How foolish I was. I am so sorry for my foolishness. Deceit can't satisfy.

'I can't serve you while I'm like this. I feel I must give up everything I'm involved in. I'm so unworthy.'

For over a year, this girl wallowed in self-pity, despair and fear that she could never be rid of the sin which had consistently stained her soul. But one day, she decided to come clean about the inner turmoil and to talk to me about it, asking: 'Do you think God could ever forgive me?'

In my experience of counselling Christians, when the root of guilt is as long as this, simply talking about forgiveness or quoting relevant verses of Scripture rarely helps. What a person needs when they are in this sort of anguish is to have the balm of the love of God applied to the sores which are still weeping inside.

'Let's ask God to show you how he feels about you', I suggested after we had talked about the nature of the sexual sin this girl had indulged in. We prayed. And I asked God to touch this girl's imagination so that she could see and hear and sense and know for herself the truth and reality and releasing power of God's liberating love.

We remained silent before God together for several minutes before I invited her to tell me what was going on in her mind. 'It's strange,' she said. 'But I've been seeing a picture of myself and Jesus.

**Forgiven, healed,
released, . . .**

PRACTICE

He showed me that I've been carrying this huge burden which is much too heavy and cumbersome for me to cope with. He showed me his big arms and asked me to let him bear the load. So I did. He took it from me. Then he said, "Come on. We're going for a walk." We walked side by side along a path that led to a lake. We stood looking at the lake for a while and then Jesus said, "Watch!" As I watched, he threw my bundle into the lake. I heard the plop, watched the ripples spread out from the place where it landed, then it was gone.

' "Gone!" That's what he said. "Your burden of sin has gone. I will remember it no more. You're free." It was such a relief. I knew it was for real. I felt so grateful. I'd do anything for him — anything. But it wasn't like talking to just any man. He was so holy. I know I have to be different from now on.'

That girl went away forgiven, healed, released, re-established and deeply challenged. It was beautiful. Such encounters with Christ are not rare, they are frequent. Jesus still aches for the Christian soiled by sexual sin. He still longs to release them. He can even restore our lost virginity.

If you, or someone close to you, needs the Holy Spirit to work deeply in this way, it is important to seek out someone who has experience in this area. It would be unwise and unkind to practise on someone's life. Better to ask a respected church member or elder who can offer wise and sensitive advice and effective prayer ministry.

A challenge

'If there's anyone who can appear before Aslan without their knees knocking, they're either braver than most or else just silly.'

'Then he isn't safe?' said Lucy.

"Course he isn't safe. But he's good. He's the king, I tell you"

C. S. Lewis, *The Lion, the Witch and the Wardrobe*, Collins, 1950

3. Receive his healing

And what of those who have been sinned against, such as victims of rape or incest? An ever-increasing number of Christians can testify to the fact that Jesus' ability to heal did not cease when he ascended. It continues. His healing love still flows into the inner hurts which have given birth to a deep-seated fear of members of the opposite sex and of God's gift of sex itself. I think of a girl who panicked when she knew I would be speaking on sex at a Christian conference she was attending. She had been raped at the age of six and could not bear even to think about the subject of sexuality.

In her panic she wrote this poem:

fear
tension in my brain
fighting for air
escape
run and hide
in the pit of shame

block out
the laughter
gasping for freedom
afraid to let go

nightmares
in my mind
flitting like ogres
in the midnight of fantasy
of hurt
and pain
that seeps
into a building
razing it
into the dust
of a million sins

. . . of the fathers
on the children . . .

hide
hide behind my mask
of excuses
that crumble
at a touch

of the pain
of a little child
crying . . .

She came to the meeting. As a result she asked for help with the memories and fears which had haunted her for years. And Jesus met her, healed her and released her from the past. She went back to her room and finished the poem:

I looked into your face
and cried to you
you heard me
you caught me as I ran
you held out your hands
in tenderness

you swamped the fear
with your love
and you held me in your arms

you are greater than tears
greater than the years
of haunting pain

you are the Lord

'Elizabeth'

This illustrates powerfully how there is hope both for those who have sinned sexually and for those who have been sinned against. Both will probably need the help of an experienced counsellor to bring them into an awareness of God's cleansing, forgiving, healing touch. But that touch still has its ancient power. The good news is that sexual sin is forgivable. Better still, many Christians today are rejoicing in the knowledge that, because of Jesus' ministry to them, the past has been dealt with. They are free.

chapter five

Should a Christian go out with a non-Christian?

"'Can we go out if he/she doesn't share my faith?'

'Should Christians go out with unbelievers?'

'Is it possible to keep a strong belief in God and make a relationship work with someone who isn't a Christian?'

'Surely, Christians should go out with unbelievers. How will they ever come to know the Lord if there is no interchange?'

'If the Bible tells us to love everyone and to share our faith with everyone, why do people say that to go out with non-Christians is wrong?'"

'Isn't there any way that Robin and I can get married, Joyce? I love him so much. I really don't want to give him up.' My heart really went out to Anna when she asked me that question because I knew that she would be devastated when I told her that, in my view, if she married Robin, her love for God and her effectiveness as a Christian would dwindle. And I understood why she became bitter when I explained this to her. 'It's as bad as belonging to a sect or something — not being able to make your own decisions, not being able to please yourself.' Peace with God only came two years later, after she had given up her relationship with Robin.

Why couldn't Anna's seemingly lovely relationship with Robin succeed? Robin was as confused about this as Anna. After all, a golf enthusiast can go out with a squash player without their relationship being impaired, and an artist can go out with a scientist and each can enrich the other. 'What's so different about a Christian going out with a non-Christian?'

Going the way of the world

The world's view on this is that it makes no difference whatsoever. For many non-Christians, it seems, relationships with the opposite sex are about making sexual conquests or enjoying a series of sex thrills. Faith and morals do not come into it. A non-Christian, who, like Robin, was a man of compassion helped me to understand this. When his Christian girlfriend accused him of forcing her to have intercourse with him, his genuine response was: 'I really am sorry. I didn't intend to hurt or insult you. I thought all girls wanted it. Why didn't you tell me Christians behave differently? I never knew!'

How could he know? He is a member of the 'Pill Generation' which recommends teenage girls to take oral contraception. He is part of a society where teenage abortions have soared to such a record level that drop-in contraceptive clinics have been opened to provide free contraceptive supplies for teenagers. He belongs to a generation which has not heard that sexual immorality is a sin.

But, as Christians, we do know that premarital intercourse is wrong. We have also pledged ourselves to live in obedience to God and his Word. So we need to ask what the Bible teaches about Christians making intimate relationships with unbelievers. Let's start with the most intimate relationship of all — marriage — because the principles involved are the same for any very close relationship.

The Bible on mixed marriages

1. Paul says 'Don't'

The Bible makes it quite clear that a Christian must not even contemplate marrying a non-Christian. Paul puts it like this: 'Do not mismate

PRINCIPLE

yourselves with unbelievers; they are not fit mates for you' *(2 Corinthians 6:14, New English Bible)*.

Or, more fully and from the *New International Version* of the Bible:

'Do not be yoked together with unbelievers . . . What does a believer have in common with an unbeliever? . . . "Come out from them and be separate, says the Lord." '

Of course, this doesn't mean 'Have nothing at all to do with non-Christians.' 'The subject-matter here is marriage with unbelievers,' claims the *New Bible Commentary*. And it is correct. Paul, like today's marriage counsellors, is exhorting Christians not to marry someone from a different faith or someone without a faith. Such relationships are now known to be high-risk propositions. This became painfully clear to me when I was counselling a married couple on one occasion. The Christian partner, the wife, was complaining bitterly about her husband. He retaliated: 'What my wife most needs is a Christian husband and I can't become a Christian just because of her.' He was right. They are now divorced. But the wife knew, when they married, that Paul says 'Don't.' She chose to be disobedient.

Jesus also says 'Don't'

It wasn't only Paul who put an embargo on mixed marriages. Jesus did too, although he does not refer to such relationships specifically. What he does do is to take us back to first principles: 'A man will leave his father and mother and be united to his wife, and the two will become one flesh' *(Matthew 19:5* quoting *Genesis 2:24)*. The oneness Jesus is referring to includes genital fusion and much more. It also means emotional oneness, creative oneness, and the spiritual oneness Adam and Eve so clearly enjoyed with each other and with God in the garden of Eden.

Marriage, as Jesus envisages it, is built on the foundation of spiritual harmony, and without a Christian partner this spiritual oneness cannot happen.

Amos says 'Don't'

Jesus' challenge reminds us of the thinking of Amos. He asked a rhetorical question: 'Do two walk together unless they have agreed to do so?' In other words: Do two form a close relationship unless they bring the same set of expectations to their developing friendship? This question is like the others which follow in *Amos 3:3-6:* 'Does a lion roar in the thicket when he has no prey? Does he growl in his den when he has caught nothing?' — questions that assume the answer 'No way'.

This verse seems to apply to friendship, business relationships and to marriage. If we are looking for a biblical perspective on the problem, therefore, we have to draw two conclusions: to marry an unbeliever is unwise and it is disobedient.

The reason for the embargo

'Why?' That was the question Anna asked me. 'Doesn't that make the so-called God of love the divine spoilsport?' Others have made similar protests. Girls complain that there just aren't enough Christian men to go around, and the ones who are there are ineligible, even 'wet'. Men complain that Christian girls are far less attractive than their non-Christian counterparts. So why is God so unreasonable?

Before we examine some of the reasons why God seems to be so insistent that Christians marry Christians, let me emphasize three truths:

1. God is not an ogre or a spoilsport. He is love. (*1 John 4:16*)

2. Love desires only the best for the loved one. (*Jeremiah 29:11*)

3. No-one is a prey of statistics. Our lives are held in the hollow of God's hand.

> **Love desires only the best for the loved one.**

The reason God instructs us to share our lives only with those with whom we are spiritually one is that he knows that otherwise we would become unhappy and dissatisfied.

PRINCIPLE

A relationship without Christ is like a vitamin-deficient diet

The Christian going out with a non-Christian suffers a kind of vitamin deficiency in the relationship. Even though other sides of the friendship may be wonderful, there will always be a spiritual lack: lack of shared prayer, lack of a united vision, lack of shared beliefs, lack of worship, lack of oneness before God, lack of ability on behalf of the Christian to share with the loved one the most precious thing that life affords: oneness with Christ.

Tensions will creep into the relationship

What is more, in the sex-saturated society in which we live, tensions will almost certainly creep into the relationship. As we saw in an earlier chapter, it takes superlative strength for two committed Christians to swim against the cultural tide. Christians have, after all, the same biological

make-up as non-Christians. How much more difficult it will be to combat the temptation to indulge in premarital sex if one of the partners sees no reason why this shouldn't happen because they owe no allegiance to Jesus. Not many of us are resolute enough or strong enough to combat such powerful anti-God influences on our own.

In a lopsided relationship, it is the Christian who usually grows cold

Many Christians have protested: 'But, surely, the non-Christian might be converted.' That is true. He or she might be. But if the statistics are to be believed, this happens only rarely. What happens most often is that the Christian partner grows cold, even cynical. That is hardly surprising when you think about it. Marrying a non-Christian is disobedience as we have seen. You can't really expect effective evangelism to be the fruit of disobedience!

. . . lack of shared prayer; of united vision; of shared beliefs and worship; lack of oneness before God.

PRINCIPLE

A friend of mine has discovered this to his cost. This friend gave his life to Christ while studying in this country. Subsequently, he returned home to resume the friendship he once enjoyed with a non-Christian girl. 'I know what the Bible says about not marrying an unbeliever. I just like her, that's all.'

But he did marry her. When I visited them in their own home, I asked him what marriage had done to his faith. A shadow seemed to pass over his face and his eyes grew sad as he admitted: 'I haven't been to church once since my wedding. I never read my Bible these days and scarcely ever pray.'

I looked out of the window and watched his small children playing in the garden. 'And the children?'

'They know nothing whatsoever about the Lord.'

'How do you feel — deep down inside, I mean?'

In reply to that question this young man admitted to the inner sadness, the yawning emptiness which no-one and nothing could fill. 'My faith really mattered to me. Jesus really mattered to me.'

This man's love for his wife has not cooled. But he has learned, the hard way, that God's instructions are both loving and wise. When we disregard them there is a price to be paid.

The unbridgeable gap

One reason for this is that the Christian has made God the Lord of his life. To the unbeliever, such a change of lordships makes not one iota of sense. It is utter foolishness. For him, there is no apparent reason why his world should not revolve around Number One, seeking pleasure, the fleeting excitements of the moment. He does not live in anticipation of the Lord's return. This is not a criticism. It is a fact. Between the Bible-observing Christian and the unbeliever, there lies an inevitable and, in some senses, an unbridgeable gulf. That is why Paul is adamant that the two should not try to entwine their lives. The incompatibility problem is as acute as trying to introduce darkness into a room which is floodlit.

You can't really expect effective evangelism to be the fruit of disobedience.

Faith divides rather than unites

These incompatibility problems pursue the couple if they marry. Their faith, rather than uniting them, divides them. And when the children come along it poses impossible questions: Shall we say grace at meals? Only when the non-Christian partner isn't around? How do we answer the children's perceptive questions, such as 'Why doesn't daddy come to church with us? Won't he go to heaven?'

Love for God cements marriages

It is not just that this man and his wife do not share the same value systems, the same guiding principles and the same beliefs. It is more than that. They are actually missing out on the riches God gives to couples who are both committed to him. God's love is like a frame which holds two human loves together. And God's love has special cementing properties. When love for God is central to two people it binds them together in a unique way. This love lies at the core of their relationship and influences everything they do and are. In such a relationship both work towards the same goal: to serve Christ, to put him first in everything, to base their lives on kingdom qualities. Their lives become integrated, creatively intertwined, harmonious. And this applies as much to the going-out phase as to marriage.

The tug-of-war

We can know all these facts in our head, but if ever we capitulate to the advances of Eros and allow ourselves to fall in love with a non-Christian we shall have the utmost difficulty in translating them into practice.

Even as I wrote this book, the phone rang. The caller was a girl whom I shall call Carol. She asked if she could come to see me. 'What's the problem?' I asked.

'Well,' she said. I know you've written all these books about relationships and I'd like to come and talk to you about mine. You see, I'm getting married in three months, but my fiancé isn't a Christian, and I'm a bit worried about it.'

'You realize you're storing up a lot of trouble for yourself, don't you?' I commented. 'Yes,' she replied. 'But I'm still going to marry him.'

C. S. Lewis explains why a committed Christian like Carol can be so blind, so stubborn and so disobedient. He talks about the passionate emotion and infatuation summed up in the Greek word *Eros*.

'It is very much the mark of Eros that when he is in us we had rather share happiness with the Beloved than be happy on any other terms. Even if the two lovers are mature and experienced people who know that broken hearts heal in the end and can clearly foresee that, if they once steeled themselves to go through the present agony of parting, they would almost certainly be happier ten years hence than marriage is at all likely to make them — even then, they would not. To Eros all these calculations are irrelevant . . . Even when it becomes clear beyond all evasion that marriage with the Beloved cannot possibly lead to happiness . . . Eros never hesitates to say, "Better this than parting. Better to be miserable with her than happy without her. Let our hearts break provided they break together." '

> **Let our hearts break — provided they break together.**

C. S. Lewis, *The Four Loves*, Fontana, 1963, p. 99

PRACTICE

By now you may be protesting. 'But I don't want someone to *marry*. I'm just wanting a boyfriend or girlfriend for a time, someone who will be 'mine' for a while. If boy-girl relationships can be good even though they don't lead to marriage, why keep concentrating on marriage?

I have placed the spotlight on the dangers of 'mixed marriages' for two reasons. First, because any relationship *might* result in marriage, and I have seen so many Christian lives wrecked by these lopsided relationships that it would be uncaring of me not to pinpoint their dangers.

And second, as I have already hinted, the principles which apply to lopsided marriages also apply to romantic relationships between Christians and non-Christians. This will become immediately obvious if you glance back at the headings in this chapter. And that is sad, because Christ loves to cement the love which holds two Christians together.

C. S. Lewis goes on to explain the nature of Eros.

The nature of Eros

1. He speaks with the authority of a god.

2. Like a demon he clamours to be honoured and obeyed.

3. He causes those in love to believe that this wonderful feeling of being utterly committed to the beloved will never ever change.

4. He persuades us to toss personal happiness on one side.

5. He plants the interests of the loved one in the centre of our being and persuades us that this is what life is about.

6. He invades and conquers every part of us: body, mind and spirit, and lures us into wanting nothing but to go on thinking about the loved one.

And, as anyone who has ever been in love will tell you, it's a wonderful feeling — like magic. It never occurs to us, though, that this feeling of euphoria and utter bliss can ever evaporate or our perspective change. But the truth is that Eros disappears just as mysteriously as he comes. He usually lingers between three and thirty-six months and then leaves a couple to face the stark reality — that 'Eros may unite the most unsuitable yoke-fellows . . . Eros may urge to evil as well as to good.' Eros prepares us for every sacrifice except the one which might be the most wise — renunciation. Eros is therefore an irresponsible master who has myriads of slaves.

No wonder it took Anna, whom I mentioned at the beginning of this chapter, years to relinquish her relationship with Robin. The inner tug-of-war for someone who really falls in love with a non-Christian will always be fierce. God longs to protect us from all this trauma and turmoil. That's why, in answer to the question 'Should a Christian marry a non-Christian?', God says a clear 'No.'

Essential questions

If you are reading this chapter because you have formed a close one-to-one relationship with an unbeliever, ask yourself these questions:

Is this relationship helping my spiritual growth or hindering it? If it is hindering your relationship with God, think carefully about these words: 'So then let us rid ourselves of everything that gets in the way, and of the sin which holds on to us so tightly, and let us run with determination the race that lies before us. Let us keep our eyes fixed on Jesus' (*Hebrews 12:1-2, Good News Bible*).

If you are over eighteen it is possible that this relationship could result in marriage. Is it responsible Christian loving to develop a close relationship with someone whom you know, under God, you cannot marry? Is it responsible to allow the friendship to deepen only to pull out at the eleventh hour, with all the hurt and turmoil that entails? Is it even responsible to dilly-dally, stringing someone along in the hope that they might become a Christian? Is that not loving yourself under the guise of loving another?

chapter six

Splitting up

PROBLEM

'When should we call it a day? Suddenly or gradually?'

'How do we actually make the break?'

'Is it inevitable that you feel sad afterwards? Is this wallowing in self-pity, or is it inevitable? How do you cope with the strength of these negative emotions?'

'Can we be just good friends afterwards?'

'How do you get over it all?'

The fickleness of Eros

You can feel madly in love with a person of the opposite sex one day, only to wake up the next, keenly aware that the bubble has burst. 'What on earth did I see in him?' you ask. 'How can I free myself from this relationship?' This is the fickleness of Eros. And he invades and conquers and bewitches Christians just as much as he overwhelms our non-Christian peers. His departure from committed Christians is also just as stealthy as his disappearance from non-Christians.

What then? When Eros has packed his bags and left a person or a couple, the two lovers are left with the reality of the situation — not the romantic' magnetism which draws them irresistibly towards one another, blinding them to almost all of each other's faults, inflaming passion for the partner; but rather leaving them with an emptiness of emotion and maybe with the horrible realization that now that Eros has gone, maybe for ever, there is little or nothing left between them.

For others life rushes on, but for you it seems to stand still.

PROBLEM

Eros beguiles us

When this happens, one or both partners might feel tremendous relief. They talk about it amicably. Even laugh. But they realize that they had become obsessed with one another and had spent an inordinate amount of time together, and that this must now change. They realize that Eros beguiles us. He persuades us that the warm, gooey feelings when we think of the loved one are signs showing us the magnanimous person that we would like to be. He hides the truth that these feelings and thrills are really signs of selfishness; that we are in this relationship, not primarily to make our partner happy, but to satisfy our own craving for intimacy and the magic of being in love. He blinds us to the fact that we may well be in love with being in love rather than being in love with a person.

Eros deceives us

When a couple finally realize these rather horrifying realities, they might decide to become 'just good friends' or they might decide to part. There need be no ill feelings on either side. Both acknowledge, albeit wryly, that the great deceiver Eros swept them, like many people before them, off their feet. Now it is time to learn from the mistakes that have been made and to return to the fulfilling challenge of rededicating all they have and are to the one they really do want to hold the reins of their life: Jesus.

Splitting up is painful

But it can happen, and often does, that Eros slips out of the back door of one partner's life while he continues to sit on the throne of the life of the other.

While the latter is still dreaming romantic dreams about the loved one, the other dreams about this particular relationship no longer. On the contrary, she (if it is the girl), realizes that, yes, he may be good-looking and generous and witty and fun to be with, but now that a shiver no longer runs down her spine when she so much as thinks of him, the relationship leaves much to be desired. In fact, it leaves her cold. She has been beguiled by infatuation rather than building a firm foundation for a lasting relationship. She knows she needs cherishing as well as cuddling. She needs someone who will take an interest in her for who she is, not just because she happens to have an attractive face or figure; someone who will share his feelings and thoughts and hopes with her as well as his amorous looks and touches; someone who stirs her spiritually as well as sexually; someone with whom she knows herself to be spiritually one. In this event, she will know that she has no alternative but to split up with her boyfriend. And in such circumstances, he may find this situation painful, even heart-breaking. He might be surprised that for several weeks he feels stunned, lost.

. . . parting is still painful. It feels like death.

It may well be that you have had a good friendly relationship which has not swept you both off your feet sexually — the ideal kind which I described earlier, in which your caring love for each other has kept in check your erotic love. Even then, it may happen that you need to part; you realize that marriage is not for you; your work perhaps takes you to opposite ends of the world. Parting is still painful. It feels like death.

A mini-death

PRINCIPLE

But this is not really surprising, because what happens when a really close relationship breaks up is that you suffer a mini-death. What follows is an experience which is very similar to the process people suffer when a loved one dies. Psychologists call it 'grief work'. At first you feel not simply stunned, but concussed. You can't take it in. It's as though you're looking at the world through double glazing and from the top of a high-rise block of flats. You see people hurrying, caught up in their busyness. For them, life rushes on. But for you, it seems to be standing still. Time drags. You become lethargic, uninterested in your

PRINCIPLE

work, careless about your appearance, apathetic about everything. Nothing matters any more. You feel lost, terribly alone. This is normal and natural.

Tears

So are tears. They are a unique kind of language expressing emotions so deep they cannot be captured by words. Tears release tension. And they are a therapy. When Jesus lost someone he loved, he wept (*John 11:35*). And he felt troubled as he faced separation from his friends (*John 14-17*).

Anger

The grief we feel when we've 'lost' someone — whether by death, or because he or she has moved to a new neighbourhood, or because we have quarrelled or split up — is rather like fear. And most people camouflage fear with anger. A certain amount of anger will almost certainly erupt, therefore. It might be anger against yourself. 'Why was I so blind? Why didn't I see that she's incapable of caring? Why didn't I detect earlier that she's selfish through and through? How could I ever be stupid enough to think that I could be married to her and be happy? I must have been a fool.' Or it might be anger against your former beloved. 'He was so callous. So cruel. The only person he ever thinks about is himself.' Or it might be the anger which expresses itself as hatred. Hatred is love hurting. So don't be surprised if you find hatred replacing the love you once had for your partner.

> **One day you may feel glad to be free. The next day your heart burns with longing.**

Searching

And you may find yourself pining and searching for your former loved one — and very reluctant to let go. Your feelings may yo-yo. One day you feel liberated, glad to be free. The next day your heart burns with longing for the return of the relationship just as it was. And when your former partner is only a telephone call away, the temptation is to pick up the phone and make contact.

First aid for broken relationships

Weep

There are several ways of coping with this jumble of emotions. The first is to weep if God gives you the gift of tears. This applies to men as well as women. Since Jesus wept, there is no need for us to be ashamed if tears come.

Be angry but do not sin

The second is to tell God about the anger and the hatred which boil up inside you. Ask him to sift it, to remove all that is sinful and to hand back to you only any anger which might be righteous. Ask him to protect you from the cancer of bitterness, to take away the hatred so that you do not lash out at others in your anger in an attempt to destroy or crush them. Ask him, too, to touch and soothe and heal your hurts. Like the good Samaritan he will come to touch your wounds and give you the strength you need to live one painful day at a time.

Angry with God?

Many people blame God for the break-up of their relationship, as if he were the cause. Here are some ways to help you through:

Tell him about it. Pour your feelings out to God and hold nothing back. He wants you to involve him in every part of your life — even your anger with him.

Listen to what he is saying. After talking, listen for an answer. Don't just put the phone down! Pray quietly that he will speak and comfort you and draw near in your pain. Be open to him and expect him to respond to your openness.

Realize he loves you. Remind yourself that his arms are stretched wide with love. He loved you enough to die for you. Sense his loving arms around you, holding you.

Trust him. A test of our spirituality is not that we understand his dealings with us but that we trust him when we don't. We trust that he does have our lives in his hands, even though we can't see his plan from where we are. 'Lord, I don't understand but I trust you.'

Don't go it alone

There is no need for any Christian to suffer the pangs of grief alone. They can be suffered with Christ. At least, that has been my experience.

As I write this, my father-in-law lies in a nursing home dying. And I am encountering two powerful emotions deep inside me: the sting of the separation which death inevitably brings, and the uncanny calm which Christ conveys as he proves his promise, 'Peace I give to you.' This experience is reminding me of my undergraduate days when I fell in love with a fellow student, another member of the Christian Union.

One cold November day he told me that 'it was not God's will' for us to go out together. I was devastated and, for a while, sipped my first taste of depression. But with the help of my room-mate's listening ear, I became conscious of the companionship of Christ in a new way.

During the long days that followed, as I looked longingly at my dashed hopes and tried to come to terms with the disappointment and humiliation, I learned a vital lesson — that aloneness need not spell loneliness. It can mature into that lovely thing called solitude.

I remember studying the Song of Solomon at that time and being stirred by God's bridegroom-love. I remember his gentle in-breathing, his tender touching of those grazed and bruised places deep inside me. Although that crisis erupted thirty years ago, I look back on it as one of the lasting landmarks of my spiritual growth. In my lostness, God found me. And to be found by him is always special.

He has not changed. I am watching similar growth take place in a very attractive young friend of mine at the moment. Her relationship with her boyfriend broke up recently. She was stunned. She cried. She was angry. She was tempted to pick up the phone just to hear his voice once more. But every week, it seems, she gives me a fresh bulletin. 'Joyce! The Lord is being so good. First he showed me how selfish I am; then he seemed to go out of his way to show me, just in little ways, how much he loves me. Now he's giving me such a close relationship with himself. Prayer is terrific.'

Turn to friends

I know it helps this girl to talk to me about her feelings just as it helped me to be able to talk about my emotions to my room-mate. God delights to use us as channels of his comfort and healing to one another. In fact, fulfilling the law of Christ by bearing one another's burdens could tip the make-or-break balance when someone's heart is in turmoil because they feel they have been battered or let down. That is why, in any situation of personal loss, it can be helpful to ask a few trusted friends to pray for you or with you. Knowing that they are supporting you in this way will release you from pressure and may well result in a much faster, more effective recovery.

The love of Christ is often best incarnated in practical ways — particularly by listening.

Or if you know of someone else who is doing the grief work I have described because their cherished relationship has broken up, be gentle, be sensitive. Love and pray them through the long tunnel until they have struggled to the sunlit mouth at the tunnel's furthest end. Don't nag or criticize or over-spiritualize, or even give advice like 'Read your Bible more;' 'What you need to do is pray.' No. Bible-reading and prayer in the Christian fellowship might not be able to touch them in the early stages. My experience is that Christlike love always wins in the end. The love of Christ is often best incarnated in practical ways — particularly by listening.

Making the break

If you know the curtain-fall is coming, it is kinder to be decisive than to dilly-dally. Most people can work through pain eventually, but living with a question mark hanging over your head creates unnecessary anxiety. 'When Jonathan came round and told me it was all over — that he was, in fact, attracted to someone else — I knew that was it. It was senseless to hope any more. He meant it. I could tell. I wept buckets and I'm

PRACTICE

afraid I was very angry, but in a funny way it helped me. I knew I had to get over it. I knew I had to get over him.'

If you are able to come to a joint decision, both agreeing that it is best to forgo the relationship, this makes the separation easier. But it often happens that one partner wants to withdraw while the other sees no reason to do so. The temptation then is to cut and run or to write a note and avoid a painful interview. And it is painful, very painful. We owe it to one another to soften the blow as much as possible.

Part of this cushioning can be done apart from the partner through prayer. Pray for him or her before, throughout and after the break-up. And part of it will be done, not by what you say, but by the way you say it. Communication experts assure us that the words we use make up a mere

7% of the message we convey, while the tone of voice contributes 38% of the message. The other 55% consists of non-verbal communication: the expression on our face, the look in our eyes, the appropriateness of our touch, the genuineness of our concern. And part of the cushioning will come through the reasons you give for pulling out of the friendship.

If you want to pull out because you are attracted to someone else, you must say so. If you want to pull out because the partnership no longer provides a springboard for serving God, you must say so. If you want to pull out because you are no longer able to give your partner the kind of love which is essential where both partners are to grow, you must say so. But be gentle, loving and decisive. Speak the truth *in love*.

> **Enjoy again the stimulus of going out with a group of people.**

PRACTICE

How do you get over it all?

1. Ask a few trusted friends to pray for you. Knowing that they are doing so will release you from pressure and may well result in a much faster, more effective recovery.

2. Make a clean breast of any mistakes you made in the relationship which leave you with a stain on your conscience or with pangs of regret.

3. Forgive yourself and your partner for any failure.

4. Recognize that there are three things you can do with the anger which flares inside you: fight the flames, run away from them, or switch off the gas. In this situation the healthiest way to cope with the anger is to recognize that there is little, if anything, that can be done about it now. Therefore, switch off the gas by handing the anger to God and let him extract what is sinful. Receive back from him only what is righteous anger. Relax.

5. Trust. In other words, acknowledge that your life and the whole of your future lie, in C. S. Lewis's memorable phrase, 'between the paws of Aslan', in other words safely in the hands of the Lord who rules the universe. Whatever comes to you next comes to you with him.

6. Make a list of the good things which the relationship gave you and thank God for them.

7. Drop your anchor back into the haven of God's presence. Enjoy the strange peace God gives even when life hurts.

8. Go back to the fellowship if you have forsaken it. You need their support.

9. Let go of the relationship as it was and the relationship as it might have been.

10. Enjoy your freedom. Make new friends. Enjoy the stimulus of group activities such as going out for the evening with several people. Rededicate your talents and time to God and ask him to use you.

This works. This was underlined for me while I was working on this chapter. I happened to bump into Anna whom I mentioned in chapter 5. She was radiant, bubbling over with joy. 'I'm happier now, Joyce, than I've ever been. I wouldn't have believed it was possible when I was going through that awful struggle — when I was resisting God and not wanting to give Robin up. But now Jesus is really the Lord of my life. I feel so free. And I'm enjoying the perks of being single. I haven't given up all thoughts of marriage though. I'm just praying that one day, soon, Mr Right will come along.'

'Make haste slowly. God's clocks keep perfect time. Live life God's way.' Anna was ready to receive those kinds of truth now. She had discovered for herself that this is the pathway to peace, contentment and lasting joy.

Frameworks talks your language

Also released:
User's guide to The Media
by David Porter

frameworks

*I*t influences everyone.

Most people watch soap operas, read a daily paper and listen to the radio but how can we enjoy them without the media manipulating our lives?

This exciting user's guide takes the lid off soaps, news, advertising and entertainment.

David Porter has contributed to *TV-AM,* the *Jimmy Young* programme, *Amateur Photographer* and the Greenbelt newspaper *Strait.*

FRAMEWORKS TALKS YOUR LANGUAGE

Kathy Keay
HOW TO MAKE THE WORLD LESS HUNGRY
– What the need is
– What's being done
– How to face the horror
– 4 Ways of making a difference.

Billy Graham and Becky Pippet
YOU HIS WITNESS
– How to share faith
– The challenge of the world
– Personal stories and advice
– Experience that works

J. John
DEAD SURE? about yourself, life, faith.
A credible explanation of Christianity for today.
– Modern problems
– Anxiety, stress, loneliness
– The Jesus story in modern English
– No resurrection – no Christianity
– Why believe?

Alan MacDonald with Tony Campolo,
Val Howard and others
THE TIME OF YOUR LIFE
– Getting more from pop and film
– Enjoying sport and friends
– Social times and social action
– The place of drink and parties

FAITH AT WORK IN TODAY'S SOCIETY

Breakout

Val Howard

Do you sometimes feel like a half-made Christian, unsure of how to live and be yourself in the church and in the world? If you do, this book is yours.

Val Howard shows how you can break out of the mould and be a real person in Christ, making a fresh and unique contribution as you mix with colleagues and friends.

She highlights, with practical examples, such areas as dress, non-verbal communication, emotion, sexuality, the use of the mind — all that goes to make you the person you are and the effective witness God intends you to be.

Val Howard was for some years an international training representative with a missionary society. She is now Corporate Marketing Manager with an international computing organization and lives in New Malden, Surrey.

160 Pages   **Pocketbook**

ivp